What church leaders say about Alpha

"What Alpha has to offer is a unique mixture of Christian content and Christian style. It isn't only about communicating what Christians believe; it communicates it in a way that becomes part of the message, showing how the teaching leads to a way of living, through friendship and hospitality. I recommend it to all the Christian family in these parts as a very special tool of evangelism."

Rowan Williams
Anglican Archbishop of Canterbury

"It is a wonderful, simple, and logical tool that may answer all the questions that one may have. It is a real introduction to the Christian story. It's great."

Canon Andrew White
Anglican Vicar of Baghdad

'"Alpha opens the door for the sharing, caring, praying community, which is exemplary of the church in action."

Desmond Tutu
Anglican Archbishop of Cape Town

"The Alpha course helps us not only to meet, love, and follow Jesus but also to help others, especially those who are lost or that have never heard about Him, to have a new start in Jesus and meet Him, love Him and follow Him, for His eternal glory."

Luis Augusto Castro
Roman Catholic Archbishop of Tunja

"I am an unequivocal lover of—and am hugely thankful in my prayers for— the work Alpha has done and is doing. I am amazed by its progress in prison. I thank God particularly for the evidence of the refreshed student work.

We have here what I believe is part of the generosity of a God who so loved the world that He gave His only Son . . . It is a method that I've seen with my own eyes . . . So you can believe me when I say: 'I've seen it, it works.'"

Richard Chartres
Anglican Bishop of London

"Alpha courses have brought many people to a living faith in Jesus Christ, and through these courses others have found a new dimension to Christian believing and belonging. I commend Alpha as one of the most exciting ventures in evangelism and basic Christian nurture in recent years. Alpha lays foundations in Christian understanding and discipleship."

John Neill
Anglican Archbishop of Dublin

"This is what I understand Alpha to be about: to know about Jesus in order that I may know Him and the power of His resurrection."

Walter P. K. Makhulu
Hon. Assistant Bishop in London

"The Alpha program has in recent years caught the imagination of a wide range of Christians. For some it has been their first contact with Christ and the faith of Christians; for others it has presented an opportunity to reconnect with their Christian faith after a period of alienation or indifference.

There is important teaching about Christ and His church, not included in the Alpha program, which the Catholic tradition would wish to add. However, I would like to commend Alpha for laying vital foundations on which others can build."

Christopher Budd
Roman Catholic Bishop of Plymouth

"The number of people going to church has doubled since we started Alpha in 2000 . . . it's a real joy to see lives transformed by Alpha."

Mouneer Anis
Anglican Archbishop of Jerusalem and the Middle East

"I am very pleased to write about the Alpha course. We live in a time when the majority of the population knows little or nothing of Christian beliefs or Christian values. The great strength of the Alpha course is that it allows genuine inquirers to take time in exploring Christian beliefs and Christian values, while building relationships with members of the church. God is using this course to lead many people to faith in Christ, to active membership of His church and to know the power of the Holy Spirit. I warmly commend it."

Graham Cray
Archbishops' Missioner

"Alpha is the most marvelous tool for evangelization. Alpha serves to bring faith alive and to me that is the most important thing in the world, because if *a person's faith and belief in Jesus becomes 'real' as opposed to 'notional' then you see the whole of life differently."*

Thomas McMahon
Roman Catholic Bishop of Brentwood

"We want to evangelize but we don't seem to have found quite the right method. I think that the Alpha course offers easily the best method so far invented. I think Alpha is very successful because it answers the questions that people are asking today. It is user-friendly. It is not a confrontational course. It is presented in everyday language. It is compelling, but no one is pressured. Above all, it enables us to come to know the Lord Jesus."

Ambrose Griffiths, OSB
Roman Catholic Bishop of Hexham and Newcastle

"The Alpha courses are transforming churches all across Britain, showing extraordinary success in stimulating interest . . . and then real faith among the uninterested and unchurched. I am so pleased to learn the courses are being introduced to the American and Canadian churches as well. A must for anyone serious about bringing others to Christ."

John W. Howe
Episcopal Bishop of Central Florida

"A priority for me on my appointment as Cardinal was the re-Christianization of Scotland. I see the Alpha course as a very important tool for this . . . An Alpha course is one of the great ways at the present time in which people can gather together to learn from one another, to share with one another, and to deepen their knowledge and love of Jesus Christ Himself."

Cardinal Keith O'Brien
Roman Catholic Archbishop of St. Andrews and Edinburgh

"Alpha is a gift from God in mission today. Its simple structure —teaching, friendship, and eating together—is borrowed from the ministry of Jesus. No wonder it works."

Graham James
Anglican Bishop of Norwich

"Alpha has proved itself to be an effective way of exploring faith and deepening commitment to Jesus as Lord. I commend it warmly."

Nigel McCulloch
Anglican Bishop of Manchester

"I believe that Alpha may well be God's instrument for salvation for many in this generation, just as Billy Graham was for so many in the previous one."

Howard Marshall
Professor Emeritus of New Testament Exegesis, University of Aberdeen

"At the heart of the gospel is both evangelism and discipleship. Alpha courses are designed to do both effectively. We have used the program in our local church with good success. I am glad to commend it."

Gordon D. Fee
Professor Emeritus of New Testament and Dean of Faculty, Regent College, Vancouver

"The Alpha course has now become one of the most reliable and important means of drawing people into the church and energizing the faith of those who are already Christians. I strongly commend this to all church leaders and congregations who are looking for ways of expanding or consolidating their ministries. Although the approach was pioneered in London, England, it can easily be adapted to anywhere in the Western hemisphere. It has enormous potential."

Alister McGrath
Professor of Theology, Ministry and Education, King's College, London

"I highly recommend the Alpha course to everyone interested in discovering how the Christian faith can be exciting and life–changing in the modern world. The course is biblically sound, understandable, and practical. It will have a significant impact on people's lives and it will strengthen every church in which it is held."

Wayne Grudem
Research Professor of Theology and Biblical Studies, Phoenix Seminary

"Alpha has pioneered a way of doing evangelism in which people are exposed both to the truths of the gospel and the power of the Spirit. Here at last is a means of communicating the gospel that does not divorce Word and Spirit."

Mark Stibbe
Director, The Father's House Trust

"For the first time I have seen a program which embodies all of the principles that many of us involved in teaching evangelism have been expounding. I am delighted that the Alpha course is coming to North America. It is making an enormous impact in the UK, being acclaimed by churches of wide-ranging traditions, as well as submitted to scrutiny in evaluating the results. As our culture becomes increasingly secularized, the insights embodied in the Alpha course will be especially appropriate."

Eddie Gibbs

Professor of Church Growth, Fuller Institute of Theology *"The phenomenal growth of Alpha courses is showing the church that we do not need to be defensive about our faith, but can expect people to be interested, and then radically changed by the gospel."*

Elaine Storkey
President, Tearfund

"We applaud the vision and work of Alpha."

Bill Hybels
Senior Pastor, Willow Creek Community Church

"It's great to see how Alpha has been used to reach people who wouldn't normally come to church with the good news of Jesus Christ. This resource is very complementary to helping seekers connect with The Purpose Driven Life.*"*

Rick Warren
Author and Pastor of Saddleback Church, California

"I know of many people whose lives have been transformed through the Alpha course. I rejoice at how God is using it so powerfully to renew many churches both inside and outside prison walls."

Charles W. Colson
Prison Fellowship Ministries

"One of the most effective tools of evangelism in the body of Christ in the United Kingdom is the Alpha course. This new and effective course has exploded, being used by hundreds of churches resulting in thousands of new believers being integrated into the local church. The enthusiasm is spreading rapidly. I wholeheartedly recommend Nicky Gumbel's excellent leadership. God has blessed the church greatly in raising up Nicky to trumpet the Alpha course."

Mike Bickle
Director, International House of Prayer

"Alpha builds churches. By taking spiritual seekers step-by-step through their unanswered questions, Alpha builds strong believers and renewed passion. That is why Alpha is such a huge success."

Bob Buford
Founder of Leadership Network

"Alpha courses are proving incredibly successful as an evangelistic format to reach people with the relevance of the gospel for our generation. The UK is being widely impacted by them and I would wholeheartedly encourage Christians in the U.S.A. to open their doors to the full impact of the ministry of Alpha."

Terry Virgo
Leader of Newfrontiers

"I have met many unlikely people from different backgrounds who have been profoundly changed through attending this course."

Jackie Pullinger
Missionary, Hong Kong and founder of the St. Stephen's Society

"Alpha is an excellent introductory course for those who do not go to church or for whom an inherited Christianity has little meaning. I have no hesitation in recommending it to any church or group wishing to present the basic gospel message clearly and effectively."

Charles Whitehead
President, International Catholic Charismatic Services

"Alpha—not just the first letter of the Greek alphabet, but first choice for an illuminating perspective on Christianity. An ideal follow-up course for missions."

J. John
Evangelist

"Alpha courses have been successfully used among our Pioneer network of churches. They are an increasing resource to those wanting to see people find forgiveness and favor in God's eyes. The course is fun and nonthreatening— just like our Lord Himself!"

Gerald Coates
Director, Pioneer Churches

"Alpha is a soul winning, discipling, multiplying, spiritually dynamic ministry that has already touched the lives of thousands. I believe this vision will continue to expand and truly become an international blessing."

Loren Cunningham
Co-founder, Youth With A Mission International

"Alpha, as developed by Nicky Gumbel and the leaders of Holy Trinity Brompton, employs all the best principles for effective evangelism—that is why it is so fruitful."

Lynn Green
International Chairman, Youth With A Mission

"The Alpha courses are being used extensively in this diocese and are proving to be an effective means of evangelism here in both urban and suburban areas. The user-friendly style is transforming many congregations and their approach to outreach."

Michael Dickens Whinney
Assistant Anglican Bishop, Diocese of Birmingham

"The great command to make disciples of all people is still relevant. Alpha provides us with contemporary cringe-free evangelism that deserves the increasing profile it is currently receiving."

Joel Edwards
General Director, Evangelical Alliance UK

"In our task of sharing the gospel as it is, with people where they are, Alpha is a creative and contemporary means of successfully doing this. I love it and think it is inspired!"

Lyndon Bowring
Executive Chairman of CARE

"Alpha is the most effective and transferable introductory course to the Christian faith that I know."

Steve Chalke
Founder, Oasis Trust

"Alpha has proved a ready and valuable tool for the churches in the eastern area as they have sought to engage in relevant and sensitive evangelism."

Paul Hills
Regional Minister, The Baptist Union of Great Britain

"The Alpha course has been of enormous value to churches in strengthening fellowship and increasing effective evangelism in the local community."

David Coffey
President, Baptist World Alliance

"The Alpha course is one of the most exciting evangelistic initiatives that has come to the church in the last decade. Don't miss it!"

Rob Parsons
Executive Director, Care for the Family

TELLING OTHERS

HOW TO RUN
THE ALPHA COURSE

NICKY GUMBEL

Published in North America by Alpha North America, 1635 Emerson Lane, Naperville, IL 60540

© 1994, 2004, 2011, Nicky Gumbel

This edition issued by special arrangement with Alpha International, Holy Trinity Brompton, Brompton Road, London SW7 1JA, UK

Telling Others: How to Run the Alpha Course
by Nicky Gumbel

Originally published by KINGSWAY COMMUNICATIONS LTD, Lottbridge Drove, Eastbourne, BN23 6NT, England

First printed by Alpha North America in 2002

Printed in the United States of America

Scripture in this publication is from the Holy Bible, New International Version (NIV), Copyright 1973, 1978, 1984, 2011 International Bible Society, used by permission of Zondervan. All rights reserved.

Scripture quotations marked [TNIV] are taken from the HOLY BIBLE, TODAY'S NEW INTERNATIONAL VERSION. Copyright © 2004 by International Bible Society. Used by permission of Hodder & Stoughton Publishers. A member of the Hachette Livre UK Group. All rights reserved. "TNIV" is a registered trademark of International Bible Society.

Illustrations by Charlie Mackesy

ISBN 978-1-933114-17-0

CONTENTS

FOREWORD

As we look around at the state of the church, the figures of declining congregations, the crumbling buildings, the general sense of failure that haunts so much of the body of Jesus Christ today, there is a temptation for many of us involved in Christian ministry to feel discouraged. St. Paul faced the same situation, yet he was able to say, "Therefore, since through God's mercy we have this ministry, we do not lose heart" (2 Corinthians 4:1).

It isn't that people are not interested in spirituality—interest in the occult, religious experiences, spiritism, and other related forms of alternative searches is as great today as ever it was—but the universal spiritual hunger, that need to fill the God-shaped hole, has not been met by those things. Our experience at Holy Trinity Brompton has been that people are now showing a new interest in the claims of Jesus Christ and the Christian faith. As our society moves into a post-Christian era many who are ignorant of the basic truth claims of Christianity are wanting to find out more about Jesus of Nazareth, especially if they can be sure of an atmosphere of acceptance, without feeling threatened, judged, or made to look foolish. I think that is one of the reasons why the Alpha course has proved to be such a success. The issues are clearly put forward and the claims of Christ examined, all in the company of other searchers and in an atmosphere of love and acceptance.

Nicky Gumbel inherited Alpha in 1990 and since then, by taking account of literally thousands of questionnaires, has adapted and improved the course so it is truly molded to the perceived and experienced needs of those who attend. Without taking anything for granted, stripping the gospel down to its bare essentials, he has made Christianity accessible to this generation.

But it is not simply hard work that has brought about the growth of Alpha. The touch of the Holy Spirit has brought the course to life from beginning to end. Hunger is created, in the hearts of those who are taking part, for the reality of God.

The Spirit alone can satisfy them. By revealing the reality of the power of Jesus Christ to forgive, to release, empower and equip, new life begins for so many who are in need of God.

At this time, there are tens of thousands of Alpha courses running throughout the U.K. and in other parts of the world. They range from small groups of five people to larger courses like the one that is running here at Holy Trinity at the moment, with over 800 people attending. Alpha is now running in 163 countries worldwide with 16 million people having completed the course.

I know that you will enjoy this book. I am confident too that by God's grace you will find many people coming into the kingdom as a result of putting into practice the principles here.

Bishop Sandy Millar
Assistant Anglican Bishop in the Diocese of London

PREFACE

Millions of people around the world are now taking part in Alpha courses—a ten-week practical introduction to the Christian faith, designed primarily for nonchurchgoers and those who have recently become Christians. In May 1993 we hosted the first Alpha conference at Holy Trinity Brompton, London, for church leaders who wanted to run such courses. Over a thousand people came, and hundreds of Alpha courses began all over the U.K. as a result. Since then we have held both regional conferences and international conferences. The number of Alpha courses in operation continues to grow daily. Having surveyed thousands of churches who are running Alpha, we have discovered that those who have attended an Alpha conference (tend to) experience a far greater degree of success on their courses. In the light of this, we strongly recommend that churches bring a leadership team to one of the numerous conferences that are held throughout the world. A list of these can be obtained from www.alpha.org.

This book is intended primarily to be a resource for churches who wish to run an Alpha course, although many of the principles of evangelism will have a wider application.

Alpha has evolved from what was essentially a basic introduction for new Christians to something that is aimed primarily at those outside the church. It was started at Holy Trinity Brompton in 1977 by Anglican clergyman Charles Marnham as a four-week course for new Christians. John Irvine took it over in 1981; he lengthened it to ten weeks and added a weekend for teaching on the person and work of the Holy Spirit. When Nicky Lee took the course on in 1985, there were about thirty-five people on each course and under his leadership that grew to well over a hundred. Since then it has grown again to over 800 people (including the leadership team) on each course (three a year). It seems sensible to pass on some of the things we have learned over the years.

In addition to the theological principles and the practical details of how courses are run, each alternate chapter consists of a testimony of someone whose life has been changed by God through an Alpha course. Each person writes in their own individual style, having recorded their experiences while the events were still fresh in their memory. Nigel Skelsey's story is taken from a letter he wrote days after his conversion to Christ. The others are based on interviews given to Mark Elsdon-Dew and originally published in *Alpha News*, of which he is the editor. He has kindly allowed me to include this material in the book.

Most of my experience has been with the evening Alpha course at Holy Trinity Brompton; in Appendix C I have included an account by Pippa Gumbel of her experience of running a daytime Alpha.

I would like to express my thanks to Jon Soper, who has acted as a researcher for this and all the other Alpha resource books. I am so grateful for his thoroughness, speed, and efficiency as well as his very perceptive comments and suggestions.

I am grateful to all the people who have read the manuscripts and offered their valuable insights and criticisms. I want to thank especially Jo Glen, Patricia Hall, Helena Hird, Simon Levell, Ken Costa, Tamsen Carter, the Rev. Alex Welby, Judy Cahusac, Nicola Hinson, Chris Russell, and Simon Downham.

Finally, a big thank you to Philippa Pearson Miles for her appendix on Administration and for typing the manuscript and organizing the project with her extraordinary combination of speed and enthusiasm, together with calmness and patience.

Nicky Gumbel

CHAPTER 1

PRINCIPLES

I am not a natural evangelist. I have never found it easy to tell others about Jesus Christ. Some people are completely natural evangelists; they find it the easiest thing in the world. I heard about one man who seizes every opportunity to talk to people about Jesus. If he is standing at a bus stop and the bus is late, he turns that situation into a conversation about the second coming! I have another friend who is a tremendously confident evangelist and speaks about Jesus wherever he goes. On a train he will speak to the person next to him about Jesus. If he's walking along the street he will turn to someone and get into conversation with them about Jesus. On one occasion when he and his family went to a Happy Eater (a popular restaurant chain at that time), he banged the table and called for silence in the restaurant. He then stood up and preached the gospel for five minutes. He says that at the end people came up to him and said, "Thank you very much, that was very helpful." I would never be able to do that.

I became a Christian on February 16, 1974. I was so excited about what had happened that I longed for everybody to follow suit. After I had been a Christian for only a few days I went to a party, determined to tell everyone. I saw a friend dancing and decided the first step was to make her realize her need. So I went up to her and said, "You look awful. You really need Jesus." She thought I had gone crazy. It was not the most effective way of telling someone the good news. (However, she did later become a Christian, quite independently of me, and she is now my wife!)

If we charge around like a bull in a china shop, sooner or later we will get hurt. Even if we approach the subject sensitively, we may still get hurt. When we do, we tend to withdraw. Certainly this was my experience. After a few years, I moved from the danger of insensitivity and fell into the opposite danger of fear. There was a time (ironically when I was at theological college) when I became fearful of even talking about Jesus to those who were not Christians. On one occasion, a group of us went from college to a parish mission on the outskirts of Liverpool, to tell people the good news. Each night we had supper with different people from the parish. One night my friend named Rupert and I were sent to a couple who were on the fringe of the church (or to be more accurate, the wife was on the fringe and the husband was not a churchgoer). Halfway through the main course the husband asked me what we were doing up there. I stumbled, stammered, hesitated, and prevaricated. He kept repeating the question. Eventually Rupert said straight out, "We have come here to tell people about Jesus." I felt deeply embarrassed and hoped the ground would swallow us all up! I realized how frozen with fear I had become and that I was afraid even to take the name of Jesus on my lips.

Ever since then I've been looking for ways in which ordinary people like me, who aren't naturally gifted evangelists, can communicate their faith with friends, family, and colleagues without feeling fearful or risking insensitivity. That is why I was so excited to discover Alpha. One simple definition of Alpha is that it is "evangelism for ordinary people."

During the 1990s the number of people attending church on an average Sunday in Britain dropped by one million, according to a survey carried out by Christian Research. By 2002, figures from the Church of England's electoral rolls showed that membership had fallen by 12 percent in a single year.[1] Despite this overall decrease, attendance among children and young people under sixteen increased by 1 percent during the same period.[2] The British Social Attitudes of 2010 suggests that over 62 percent of the population never attend any form of church service. By 2015, the level of regular church attendance is predicted to fall to just over 3 million people. The vast majority of the population of the United Kingdom do not attend church, and of those who do, many only go at Christmas or Easter. Following in the wake of the decline in Christian belief, there has been a decline in the moral climate. The fabric of our society is unravelling. Every day in Britain at least 330 couples are divorced, twenty babies are born to teenage mothers under the age of sixteen and 518 babies are aborted. If the divorce rate is falling, this is only because fewer people are getting married, and half of all couples divorcing have at least one child under the age of sixteen. In addition, at least one new crime is committed every six seconds and a violent attack takes place every nine minutes. In the late 1990s, while there were 30,000 Christian clergy of all types, there were more than 80,000 registered witches and fortune tellers.[3]

But at the same time, shoots of new life are springing up all over the place. New churches are being planted and many established churches are seeing growth, sometimes slow and sometimes quite dramatic. Many Christian initiatives that arose out of the renewal movement in the Decade of Evangelism continue to build and encourage the church. One of those new shoots is the Alpha course. All of us involved with it have sensed the extraordinary blessing of God upon it.

I realize that we need to be cautious about saying this is a work of God. I know the story of the man who came up to a preacher and said, "That was a great talk." The preacher rather piously replied, "It wasn't me, it was the Lord," to which the man responded, "It wasn't that good!" In saying that we believe Alpha is a work of God I am not for a moment suggesting that it is perfect. I'm sure that it is greatly marred by human error and frailty. There is much room for improvement and we try to listen carefully to constructive criticism. Nor do we believe that it is the only method of evangelism that God is blessing: far from it. Nevertheless, all the signs point to it being an extraordinary work of God and we are deeply grateful.

When Alpha first started growing I thought, "How could something that started in Central London work elsewhere?" Alpha currently runs in more than 163 countries including: Zimbabwe, Kenya, Norway, Denmark, Sweden, Germany, Malaysia, Hong Kong, Australia, New Zealand, Japan, India, Korea, the United States, Canada and many others.

While at an Alpha conference in Zimbabwe, I discovered that Alpha was not only running among the English-speaking white Zimbabweans but also among the Shona-speaking people in their own language. Zimbabwe has a population of almost 12.5 million people: there are around 70,000 whites in Zimbabwe but over 6 million black Zimbabweans speak Shona. While I was at the conference I met a man called Edward Ngamuda. He had originally done Alpha in English but then thought that he would like to run the course in Shona. A couple, who had come to Christ on Alpha, owned a farm with 900 workers. They asked him to come and run the course for those who worked on their farm. Thirty people came on the first course and fifty came on the second. I asked him whether these people were Christians when they came on the course. "No," he replied, "we had a Muslim, a witchdoctor, and a polygamist come." I asked how the polygamist happened to be there and was told that his first wife came on the first course, and that she had brought him and the other two wives on the next one! Edward assured me that Alpha worked better in Shona than it did in English. It was then that I began to realize that this course, which started in London, could operate in different countries and cultures. Why is this?

I believe it is because Alpha is based on six New Testament principles; in this first chapter, I want to look at each of these principles in turn.

Evangelism[4] is most effective through the local church

I'm ashamed to say that when I used to think of evangelism, I only thought of two types. I thought of mass evangelism: Jesus spoke to crowds; Paul spoke to crowds—and that has a good history in the church. I also thought of personal evangelism: Philip with the Ethiopian and Jesus with the woman at the well. But what I had never noticed was that in the New Testament the dominant model is evangelization through the local Christian community. Paul wrote to the Christians at Thessalonica and he said: "The Lord's message rang out from you" (1 Thessalonians 1:8)—that is, from the local Christian church.

John Stott, author of many books and Rector Emeritus of All Souls, Langham Place, has described evangelism through the local church as "the most normal, natural, and productive method of spreading the gospel today."[5] Similarly, in March 1998 at the U.S. Bishops' Ad Limina address, Pope John Paul II affirmed that the parish will necessarily be the center of the new evangelization. There are at least four reasons for this.

What you see is what you get

Missions and Billy Graham-style crusades clearly have been greatly used by God. They raise the profile of the church and are still an effective means of bringing people to Christ. In our church we often take teams on missions to universities and elsewhere and we appreciate the value and fruitfulness of this type of evangelism. But missions are more likely to bear lasting fruit if they are earthed in an ongoing program of local church evangelism, because they then have the great advantage of continuity of relationships. Someone may respond at a crusade or mission and be referred to their local church. They may be disappointed to find the environment of the church radically different from the meeting that attracted them in the first place and so they subsequently stop attending. This is one of the reasons why the follow-up after big crusades is so hard. By contrast, if someone is introduced to Christianity at their local church, they become familiar with the place and the people, and are therefore much more likely to stay. We are finding on Alpha that belonging comes before believing for many people.

I used to think that people would come to faith and then join a local church—that believing would come first and then belonging. Those who come on an Alpha course don't think they are joining the church; they are coming to explore the Christian faith. And at one level that is all Alpha is: it is an opportunity to explore the meaning of life. But then over the weeks they start to make friends with the other people in the group, and they start to look forward to seeing each other. In a recent small group, one person said, "Well, you know, my father is a Muslim. I don't really know what I am." Another said, "Well, I haven't been to church since I went to chapel at school." Another one said, "You know, I've *never* been to church. I was brought up as an atheist." At the end of the evening they all went off to have a drink together, because they had become friends. This way, when guests such as these come to faith they are already part of a Christian community —part of a local church. Without really noticing it, they have started by belonging and then, in many cases, they have come to believe. This is what makes it so much easier to integrate them into the church.

Incidentally, no one *joins* Alpha—Alpha does not have a single member. They join their local church. If a guest does Alpha in our parish, they join the parish church here. If they do it in a Catholic church in Latin America, they join the Catholic church in Latin America. If they do it in a church in China, they join the Chinese local church. This is one of the reasons why all these different parts of the church are happy to run the course: because they know that if they run it in the Coptic Orthodox Church, the guests will join the Coptic Orthodox Church. If they run it in the Baptist Church, they join the Baptist Church. So belonging comes before believing. What they see when they come is what they're going to get.

It mobilizes a whole army of evangelists

In every church there are people who have gifts that can be used in evangelism, but often their gifts are not utilized. For example, a Gallup survey discovered that only 10 percent of American church members are active in any kind of personal ministry. However, an additional 40 percent expressed an interest in having a ministry, but did not know how to start. This group is an untapped gold mine.

What we find on Alpha is that we are mobilizing people who have the gift of evangelism. People come on the course as a guest and many of them (though not all) come to faith in Christ. We don't allow these new Christians to come back and repeat the course, but they can come back as a helper as many times as they like. We generally don't allow them to repeat the course because we don't want the course full of people who have done the course over and over again. It would be very off-putting for new guests, apart from anything else, to do the introductions on the first night: "How do you come to be on Alpha?" "Well, this is my fifth Alpha course." We call those people *Alphaholics*. We try instead to involve them in a different ministry in the church.

What does work well is when they first come on the course as a guest, then they come back as a helper on a few Alpha courses. Then they might even eventually go on to host a small group or take that group on to form a new home group, or cell group, in the church.

Take, for example, Hailey, twenty-two years of age. She came on the course two years ago: not a churchgoer; not a Christian. She came to faith in Jesus Christ on the Alpha weekend and immediately started talking to some of her colleagues at work, and they started asking her questions. She came to me in about Week 7 of the course and said, "Do you know, I don't know the answer to any of their questions! They keep asking me, "What about other religions? What about suffering?" So I said, "Well, do you have a Christian friend that you could go to? Do you have anyone at work who is a Christian?" She said, "No, I don't think there are any other Christians at work." I said, "Well, do you have any Christian friends from university?" She said, "No, I don't think I met anyone at university who was a Christian." I said, "What about school—did you meet any Christians at school?" She said, "No, I don't think I met any Christians at school." I said, "Have you ever met a Christian before in your life?" She said, "No, I don't think I've ever met a Christian before in my life." This is England! But she came to faith, and so we asked her to come back and help on the next course. She was an excellent helper.

We find that people who did the previous course are the best helpers, because they're a kind of bridge. When the guests come, they're able to say to them, "Look, I was in your position three months ago. I understand totally how you feel." They speak their language and so they identify with them. On the following course Hailey hosted the small group. She had only been a Christian six months but she made an excellent small group host.

On every Alpha course, approximately one-third of the people involved are hosts and helpers; all of them are doing evangelism. Tens of thousands of people are now involved. Steve Morgan, the Rural Dean of Merthyr Tydfil in South Wales, put it like this:

> It has been the heart cry of past generations to put evangelism within the grasp of ordinary people who are terrified at the thought of evangelism. This has never happened before. We have here "a history-making thing." For generations, the only people who would touch evangelism were those with an outgoing
> personality. But now the shy little old lady can embrace evangelism for the first time. It has never been available for all types of personality before. Any church, at any time, with any group can run with this. We believe that the nation has been praying and calling out for this for generations.

It is friendship based
Alpha is a New Testament model of evangelism: Peter brought his brother Andrew; Philip brought his friend Nathaniel; the woman at the well went back and told everyone in her town; and Matthew the tax collector threw a party and invited all his work colleagues to meet Jesus. Pope Benedict XVI said, "Anyone who has discovered Christ must lead others to Him.

A great joy cannot be kept to oneself. It has to be passed on."[6]

Alpha is a form of *come and see* evangelism. What happens is people come to Christ, they get excited about Jesus and they say to their friends, "Come and see!" This is why Alpha works best with people outside the church. However, what we found as other churches started to run Alpha was that not all of them used it for people outside the church. Instead, they would start an Alpha course for people who were members of the church and as a result they would have a big first Alpha course—perhaps fifty people on the first course. By the second course, they were running out of people in the church: down to twenty-five. Third course, they'd virtually run out of church members: down to five people. And they thought, "Alpha's not working. The numbers are declining." What they hadn't realized was that Alpha hadn't started: all that had happened was it had been introduced to the church. There's nothing wrong with that at all, but that's not Alpha. Alpha is designed for people *outside* the church. Sadly, some churches have given up at that point. For other courses, out of those five people on the course there might have been one person—a fringe person—who came to faith in Jesus, was filled with the Spirit, got excited about Jesus and brought their friends on the next course. And some of *them* came to Christ and they brought *their* friends on the next course. As a result, the course is now growing. This is Alpha.

The pattern of Alpha is that people come to Christ and are filled with the Spirit. They then realize the wonder, the importance, and the relevance of what God has done for them through Christ and they want to tell their friends, family, and work colleagues. Most of these others probably do not go to church nor are they Christians. Some of these in turn come and do the course. Some of them come to Christ, and are filled with the Spirit. They too become excited about Jesus and tell *their* friends, family, and colleagues. In this way we find that we are constantly breaking into new circles of unchurched people.

The more checkouts, the more customers
One big evangelistic crusade may bring great blessing but it is limited both in time and space. If every local church in the world was running an effective ongoing program of local church evangelism and every month people were coming to Christ and bringing their friends and

these friends then brought other friends—imagine how quickly the world would be reached for Christ!

Michael Green, Advisor in Evangelism to the Archbishops of Canterbury and York, summed up the need for this kind of evangelism in his book *Evangelism Through the Local Church*:

> Whenever Christianity has been at its most healthy, evangelism has stemmed from the local church, and has had a noticeable impact on the surrounding area. I do not believe that the re-Christianization of the West can take place without the renewal of local churches in this whole area of evangelism. We need a thoughtful, sustained, relevant presentation of the Christian faith, in word and in action, embodied in a warm, prayerful, lively local church which has a real concern for its community at all levels . . . Such evangelism, in and from the local church, is not only much needed but . . . eminently possible. I believe it to be the most natural, long-lasting, and effective evangelism that is open to us. If local churches were engaging in loving, outgoing evangelism within their neighborhoods, many of our evangelistic campaigns, missions, and crusades would be rendered much less necessary.[7]

Evangelism is a process

Conversion may take place in a moment but it is part of a process. Jesus used the expression "born again" (John 3:3) for the beginning of a spiritual life, and the New Testament speaks about becoming a child of God. While the birth of a child may be one event, there is a much longer process before and afterwards. The Bible uses many other images to represent spiritual growth: some are taken from agriculture, others from the ideas of building or journeying. All of these involve a process. That is why, in many ways, I prefer the word "evangelization" used mainly by Roman Catholics, as it seems to reflect the New Testament understanding of conversion as the start of the Christian life.

Alpha is a ten-week course involving a total of fifteen talks, which include a weekend mid-way through the course, and a celebration party at the end. We do not expect people to respond to the gospel after the first week (although some do). We recognize that people need time to think, watch, listen, and to talk through their questions and difficulties. Each person is beginning at a different stage.

Some are already Christians but will often say, in retrospect, that at the start of the course they were Christians "without any real experience of God." Others are at the point of new birth when they begin Alpha. Some have already given their lives to Christ at the party at the end of the previous course, others at a guest service before the beginning of Alpha. Still others perhaps come to faith through the witness of their family or a friend. Many are still a long way off when they begin Alpha. Some are convinced atheists, some are "New Agers," some are adherents to other religions or cults. Many are living in lifestyles that are far from Christian. Some are alcoholics, others are compulsive gamblers, many are living with partners they are not married to and some are in a homosexual lifestyle. We welcome them all. Some will complete the whole course and still not be Christians at the end; we hope they will be unable to say they have not heard the gospel. Others will give their lives to Christ at some stage on the course. For nearly all of them, Alpha will enable them to take a step forward in their relationship with God.

The fact that there is a process spread over fifteen sessions enables us to give longer to aspects of the Christian faith than one would be able to in one evangelistic talk. It is a process of understanding. For example, in 1994 I saw a man standing at the back of the room who looked very suspicious and worried. When I introduced myself he said, "I don't want to be here, I've been dragged along." I said, "Great! Let me introduce you to eleven other people who don't want to be here," and I took him to meet my small group. At the end of the evening I heard him chatting to someone else in the group.

"Are you coming back next week?"

The other man replied, "Yes, I'll be here."

To which the first man said, "Well, if you're coming back next week, I'll come back next week."

Six weeks later he said to me, "This course is like a jigsaw puzzle. Every time I come back another piece fits into place. And I'm beginning to get the picture."

Furthermore, the fact that Alpha is a process enables trust to develop. One national survey in the U.S. asked people to rank various professions for their honesty and integrity. TV evangelists came close to the very bottom, below lawyers, politicians, car salesmen, and prostitutes. Out of the seventy-three occupations compared in this survey, only two ended up lower on the scale: organized crime bosses and drug dealers. There is a great deal of cynicism, scepticism, and distrust about the Christian church. I had no idea of the extent of this until I spoke to someone who said that for the first three weeks of the course he had not eaten the food in case it was drugged. That was an extreme case of distrust but many other people wonder if the church is after their money, their mind, or something else. It can take a few weeks for a level of trust to build. As the guests get to know their small group hosts, they begin to see that they are not "after" anything and they start to listen.

Evangelism involves the whole person

Evangelism involves an appeal to the whole person. Pope John Paul II, speaking to bishops from Japan, said that "evangelization . . . must touch people's minds and hearts, stir their consciences, and engage all their energies." Indeed, each talk on Alpha is designed to appeal to the mind, heart, conscience, and will, although in some of the talks the emphasis will be on just one of those aspects.

We appeal to the mind because we believe that Christianity is based in history: on the life, death, and resurrection of Jesus Christ. We preach "Jesus Christ and him crucified" (1 Corinthians 2:2). We seek to persuade with every argument we can muster, just as Paul did on so many occasions (e.g., Acts 18:4). We try to teach only what we can establish from the Bible and we point people to the biblical text. We do not expect anyone to take a "blind leap" of faith. Rather, we hope they will take a step of faith based on reasonable grounds.

Second, we appeal to the heart. St. Paul writes in Romans 5:5, "God has poured out his love into our hearts by the Holy Spirit, who has been given to us." [TNIV]. Our message does not simply require

an assent of the intellect to a series of propositions; rather it calls people to a love-relationship with Jesus Christ. John Stott has written:

> There is a place for emotion in spiritual experience. The Holy Spirit's . . . ministry is not limited to illuminating our minds and teaching us about Christ. He also pours God's love into our hearts. Similarly, he bears witness with our spirit that we are God's children, for he causes us to say "Abba, father" and to exclaim with gratitude, "How great is the love the father has lavished on us, that we should be called children of God!" . . .
>
> I think it was Bishop Handley Moule at the end of the last century who gave this good advice: "Beware equally of an undevotional theology (i.e., mind without heart) and of an untheological devotion (i.e., heart without mind)."[8]

Graham Cray, Archbishops' Missioner, has spoken with great insight about the contemporary culture, which is in the process of shifting from an Enlightenment culture to a new and coming one. In the Enlightenment, reason reigned supreme and explanation led to experience. In the present transitional culture with its "pick-and-mix" worldview, in which the New Age movement is a potent strand, experiences lead to explanation.

Pope John Paul II, speaking to young people in Italy, asked them this: "If your faith is not based on experience, how can you account for your hope to yourselves and others? How can you overcome the doubts and crises that are so characteristic of your age? Open the doors of your hearts to the experience of the Lord." I have often found that many older people approach Alpha from an essentially Enlightenment perspective. They feel at home with the parts of the course that appeal to the mind, but often have difficulty in experiencing the Holy Spirit. Others, often the younger guests coming from the New Age movement, find that rational and historical explanations leave them cold, but at the weekend away they are on more familiar territory in experiencing the Spirit. Previously they will have been seeking experiences, which have then left them discontented and only in experiencing a relationship with God through Jesus Christ do they find their hunger is satisfied.

The gospel involves both the rational and the experiential and it impacts both those from an Enlightenment background who need to experience God and those who have sought experiences but who need to understand the truth about God.

Third, we seek to appeal to the conscience. Paul writes, "By setting forth the truth plainly we commend ourselves to everyone's conscience in the sight of God" (2 Corinthians 4:2). We know that every person has a conscience. Deep down we all have a sense of right and wrong. The Holy Spirit, often working through people's conscience, convinces them about sin. Their consciences therefore are on our side. Throughout the course we are appealing to this side in urging people to repent and turn to Christ.

Fourth, we seek to appeal to the will. We recognize, of course, that no one can come to the Father unless God calls them. As Jesus said, "No one knows the Son except the Father, and no one knows the Father except the Son and those to whom the Son chooses to reveal him" (Matthew 11:27). On the other hand, Jesus went on to say in the very next verse, "Come to me, all you who are weary and burdened, and I will give you rest" (Matthew 11:28). In other words, He called for a decision.

The apostle Paul sought to reason with people; he sought to prove that Jesus was the Christ. He said, "we try to persuade people" (2 Corinthians 5:11). But, there is a big difference between an appeal to the will (persuasion) and pressure. We try to avoid all forms of pressure on Alpha. We do not endlessly exhort anyone to respond, or chase after people if they do not come back: it is up to them to decide. Over the period of ten weeks, as we pray and allow the Holy Spirit to do His work, giving people the opportunity to respond, we are, in effect, making a continuous appeal to their wills.

Sometimes people have said to me, "Surely that is unbiblical! Surely we ought to go chasing after them." And my answer would be, well, I'm not sure it *is* unbiblical—at that point in their life. Take the example of Jesus with the rich young ruler. Do you know, Jesus dealt with the rich young ruler so differently from the way in which I would have been tempted to deal with him. The rich young ruler came to Jesus, and Jesus said: "If you want to become a follower of mine, this is what you have to do." And the rich young ruler said, "I can't do that." And he went away sorrowful. Jesus loved him, but He did not go running after him.

And people *do* drop out and it is very disappointing. Sometimes they drop out after maybe just one week and you think, "Should I have gone chasing after that person? It's so sad that they never came back." But you never ever know what's happened.

I play a lot of squash and I belong to a club. Once when I was playing squash, I looked up and saw a face I kind of recognized. So I said, "Hi!" Then, when I was in the gym afterwards, the same man came up to me and he said, "Nicky Gumbel?" And I said, "Yes." He introduced himself—his name was Tom. He had been in our small group on Alpha but he had only come once—that was it. I remembered him because he was a very interesting guy, and I had been really disappointed that he dropped out. But, standing in the gym, he said to me, "You know, it was that night fifteen years ago that totally changed my life." The talk that evening was "Why Did Jesus Die?", and he'd understood the message, and he had an experience of Jesus Christ. I'm yet to discover why he didn't come back, but fifteen years later he's still following Jesus. You never know.

Models of evangelism in the New Testament include classical, holistic, and power evangelism

Graham Tomlin, Principal of St. Mellitus theological college in London, draws attention to three different models of evangelism.[9] Clearly these three are not mutually exclusive and we very much hope that the Alpha course involves all three models.

Classical evangelism – words

First there is *classical evangelism*, which involves "the proclamation of the unchanging message." Certainly, at the heart of Alpha is the proclamation of the gospel of Jesus Christ: the first talk is about Christ's deity, the second is about his death on the cross for us and each talk has at its core some principle of Christian belief and living. Essentially, it is *Alpha*; it's not Alpha, Beta, Gamma, Delta through to Omega. It's *Alpha*—the beginning. They have the rest of their lives for Beta, Gamma, Delta through to Omega—there is lots to learn afterwards. But on Alpha it's the proclamation of the *kerygma*, the basic message of Jesus Christ, Him crucified, risen from the dead.

We do not believe we have the liberty to tamper with the apostolic message. However, the message comes to us in a cultural packaging. Every generation has a duty to ensure that the packaging is not a stumbling block; to preserve the unchanging message but to change the packaging in order to make it understandable in the context of their own culture. Martin Luther translated the Scriptures into the German vernacular, and the Lutheran Church adapted the folk music of the day into songs of worship. The Methodist Church under the leadership of the Wesley brothers "agreed to become more vile to reach the common people and to speak in the most obvious, easy, common words, wherever our meaning can be conveyed." General William Booth, the founder of the Salvation Army, memorably said, "Why should the devil have all the good tunes?"

Pope John Paul II put it like this: "The new evangelization demands that you present, with . . . new methods, the eternal and unchanging context of the heritage of our Christian faith."[10] In a similar vein Pope Paul VI wrote:

> On us particularly, the pastors of the Church, rests the responsibility of re-shaping with boldness and wisdom, but in complete fidelity to the content of evangelization, the means that are most suitable and effective for communicating the gospel message to the men and women of our times . . . The individual Churches . . . have the task of assimilating the essence of the gospel message and of transposing it, without the slightest betrayal of its essential truth, into the language that those particular people understand, and then of proclaiming it in this language.[11]

Holistic evangelism – works

Second, there is *holistic evangelism*. As John Stott wrote, "We are convinced that God has given us social as well as evangelistic responsibilities in his world."[12]

Evangelism and social action go hand in hand. The latter involves both social justice in the removal of injustice, inhumanity, and inequality; and social service in relieving human need, such as hunger, homelessness, and poverty. Evangelism and social action both stem from the love of God. If we love people, we want them to know about Jesus. If we love people, we want them to have food, we want their diseases to be cured, we want them to have universal primary education, we want the homeless to have a roof over their heads.

And one of the first things we did here was to start a homeless shelter: we have a day shelter; we also have a night shelter. Thirty-eight men and women sleep overnight in the church during the winter months. One of the first people to walk in was "Big John." He came with his friend, "Little John." Big John, at forty-nine years of age, had all his teeth missing and had been sleeping on the streets of London for eleven years. He had spent the previous ten years in prison. The first thing that struck him at the night shelter was the team of young people who were looking after him: they fed him; they gave him a manicure; they cut his hair; they cared for him; they loved him.

Big John was so amazed by this he said, "Look, I want to come to church on Sunday, just to say thank you to you." So he turned up at church the following Sunday and he loved it. He heard about Alpha, because we were advertising the start of the next Alpha course, and he said, "I want to come on the Alpha course." So he attended Alpha, went on the Alpha weekend and on the Saturday night of the weekend he gave his life to Christ. Big John was filled with the Holy Spirit and instantly came off what was quite a heavy dose of drugs. He was a changed man. He even began to *look* different, and his friends noticed the difference on the streets.

The first thing we did was to try to find him somewhere to live. We called around to all the different real estate agents but none of them wanted to help. They said, "We don't take people like that." Eventually, we called a real estate agent and a man answered the phone. And Cat, who was calling around, said, "This is Cat from Holy Trinity Brompton." "Oh," he said, "I know Holy Trinity Brompton—I go there! How can I help you?" She said, "Well, we're trying to find accommodation for someone who's been homeless." And this man said, "What's his name?" And she said, "Well, his nickname is Big John." He said, "I know Big John—I was on the same Alpha weekend as him." This real estate agent had been an atheist two years ago. He came to a service at HTB and there was a word of knowledge, which he responded to—his name is Will Wisbey and he was the manager of that agency. He didn't pick up the phones normally but, on this occasion, there was no one in the room, so he had picked it up. He said, "I played table tennis with Big John on the Alpha weekend! I'll help him." And we found him somewhere to live. A dentist then volunteered to fix his teeth—it would have cost thousands of pounds.

Those that had known Big John from the streets saw the change in him, and he started to bring them to church. He would say to them, "Look, guys, you don't realize what you're missing out on! You've got to come to church with me!" And each week he would bring a different group of homeless people with him. His nickname on the streets of London changed from Big John to John the Baptist! He has been a helper on the Alpha course and is a totally different man.

We had a visit from HRH Prince Charles, who came to see some of the work we do in the parish, and one of the people we introduced him to was Big John. And now Big John's mother—who hadn't seen her son for many years—proudly has a picture on her wall of her son with Prince Charles. That is Jesus changing people's lives. That is holistic evangelism.

We attempt on Alpha to avoid the dangers of pietism by our teaching and example, believing that evangelism is fundamentally linked to social responsibility. As Bishop Lesslie Newbigin put it:

> Christian programs for justice and compassion . . . severed from their proper roots in the liturgical and sacramental life of the congregation . . . lose their character as signs of the presence of Christ and risk becoming mere crusades fueled by a moralism that can become self-righteous. And the life of the worshiping congregation, severed from its proper expression in compassionate service to the secular community around it, risks becoming a self-centered existence serving only the needs and desires of its members.[13]

Power evangelism – wonders

Third, there is *power evangelism*, where the proclamation of the gospel goes hand in hand with a demonstration of the Spirit's power (1 Corinthians 2:1–5). We include this third element because we believe it is firmly based in New Testament practice.

It used to be argued that you cannot take doctrine from narrative, but New Testament scholars have shown to the satisfaction of theologians of all varieties that the Gospel writers were not only historians, they were theologians as well. In a different literary form, they were writing theology as much as Paul or the other writers of the New Testament epistles. In the Gospels, the central theme in the teaching of Jesus is the kingdom of God. The coming of the kingdom involved not only the spoken proclamation of the gospel but also a visible demonstration of its presence by signs, wonders, and miracles. Each of the Gospel writers expected these to continue.

We can see this from the way in which Matthew sets out his Gospel. He tells us that "Jesus went throughout Galilee, teaching in their synagogues, preaching the good news of the kingdom, and healing every disease and sickness among the people" (Matthew 4:23). He then gives some of the teaching and preaching of Jesus in chapters 5–7 (the Sermon on the Mount), then nine miracles (mainly of healing) and he concludes with an almost exact repetition of Matthew 4:23: "Jesus went through all the towns and villages, teaching in their synagogues, preaching the good news of the kingdom and healing every disease and sickness" (Matthew 9:35). Matthew is using a literary device of repetition known as an "inclusio," a short piece of text which appears at the beginning and at the end of a particular section and which acts as punctuation by enclosing a theme. Having shown what Jesus Himself did, Matthew tells us that Jesus then sent the Twelve out to do the same. He told them to go out and preach the same message: "As you go, preach this message, 'The kingdom of heaven is near.' Heal the sick, raise the dead, cleanse those who have leprosy, drive out demons" (Matthew 10:7–8).

At the end of his Gospel, Matthew makes it clear that Jesus expected all his disciples to "go and make disciples of all nations . . . teaching them to obey *everything* I have commanded you" (Matthew 28:19–20, italics mine). This surely includes not only His ethical teaching, but also the earlier commissions.

In Mark's Gospel we see a similar pattern. Mark tells us that Jesus proclaimed the good news (Mark 1:14 onwards), demonstrating it by signs and wonders (Mark 1:21 onwards). The kingdom of God was inaugurated by Jesus and is still growing to this day. There is no reason why its fundamental nature should have changed. Indeed, in the longer ending of Mark (which is, at the very least, good evidence of what the early church believed Jesus' commission to be), Jesus said, " 'Go into all the world and preach the good news to all creation . . . and these signs will accompany *those who believe*: In my name they will drive out demons . . . they will place their hands on sick people, and they will get well . . .' Then the disciples went out and preached everywhere, and the Lord worked with them and confirmed his word by the signs that accompanied it" (Mark 16:15–20, italics mine). Jesus says, "These signs will accompany *those who believe*"—that is to say, those who believe in Jesus Christ, which means all Christians.

For Luke's theology we need to look at both Luke and Acts. Luke tells us in his Gospel: "When Jesus had called the Twelve together, he gave them power and authority to drive out all demons and to cure diseases, and he sent them out to preach the kingdom of God and to heal the sick" (Luke 9:1–2). Nor was it only the Twelve to whom He gave this commission; He also appointed seventy-two others and told them to go out and "heal the sick who are there and tell them, 'The kingdom of God is near you' " (Luke 10:9).

In the book of Acts this continues beyond the time Jesus was on earth. After the outpouring of the Holy Spirit, there is a remarkable continuation of supernatural power, ranging from speaking in tongues to raising the dead. These demonstrations of power continue right through to the last chapter (Acts 28:7–9). In the Acts of the Apostles we see the outworking of this commission. The disciples continued to preach and teach, but also to heal the sick, raise the dead, and cast out demons (Acts 3:1–10; 4:12; 5:12–16; 8:5–13; 9:32–43; 14:3, 8–10; 19:11–12; 20:9–12; 28:8–9).

Nor is this ministry in the Spirit's power confined to the synoptic Gospels. In John's Gospel Jesus is recorded as saying, in the context of miracles, "All who have faith in me will do the works I have been doing, and they will do even greater things than these, because I am going to the Father" (John 14:12, TNIV). Clearly no one has performed miracles of greater quality than Jesus, but there has been a greater quantity since Jesus returned to the Father. He has not ceased to perform miracles, but now He uses weak and imperfect human beings. Again it says, "All who have faith in me:" that is, all Christians. These commands and promises are not restricted anywhere to a special category of people.

Signs and miracles were a central part of Paul's proclamation of the gospel (Romans 15:19). It is also clear from 1 Corinthians 12–14 that Paul did not believe that such abilities were confined to the apostles and he expected the more obviously supernatural gifts of the Spirit to continue in an effective and healthy church. He speaks about "gifts of healing," "miraculous powers," "prophecy," "speaking in different kinds of tongues," and "the interpretation of tongues." He described these as being given to different members of the body of Christ and as being the work of the Spirit (1 Corinthians 12:7–11).

Nowhere in the New Testament does it say that these gifts will cease at the end of the apostolic age. On the contrary, Paul says that they will only cease when "perfection comes" (1 Corinthians 13:10). Some have identified "perfection" here with the formation of the canon of Scripture, saying that as we now have the Bible, we have no need of "imperfect" spiritual gifts. However, the context for this verse clearly shows that Paul is identifying "perfection" with the return of Jesus. The world is not yet perfect, neither do we see Jesus "face to face" (v. 12), nor do we "know fully" (v. 12) but we know only "in part" (v. 12). This "perfection" will only occur when Jesus returns and then these gifts will no longer be necessary. Until that moment they are a vital part of the church's armory. Indeed, this passage shows that Paul did not expect the gifts to cease until the return of Jesus.

Likewise, the writer to the Hebrews says that God testified to His message by "signs, wonders and various miracles, and gifts of the Holy Spirit" (Hebrews 2:4). Nowhere in the Bible is the supernatural display of the power of the Holy Spirit confined to any particular period of history. On the contrary, such signs, wonders, and miracles are part of the kingdom which was inaugurated by Jesus Christ and continues to this day. Hence we should expect today to see the supernatural display of the power of the Holy Spirit as part of His kingdom activity and as an authentication of the good news. However, we do not draw ultimate attention to the signs and wonders, but to the God of love who performs them.

Evangelism in the power of the Holy Spirit is both dynamic and effective

On the day of Pentecost such was the power with which Peter preached that the people were "cut to the heart" and 3,000 were converted (Acts 2:37–41). The remarkable events continued: "Everyone was filled with awe, and many wonders and miraculous signs were done by the apostles . . . And the Lord added to their number daily those who were being saved" (Acts 2:43–47).

Remarkable healings followed (Acts 3:1–10). People were astonished and came running to find out what had happened (3:11). Peter and John preached the gospel with great boldness: "When they saw the courage of Peter and John and realized that they were unschooled, ordinary men, they were astonished and they took note that these men had been with Jesus. But since they could see the man who had been healed standing there with them, there was nothing they could say" (Acts 4:13–14). The authorities had no idea what to do because "all the people were praising God for what had happened. For the man who was miraculously healed was over forty years old" (Acts 4:21–22).

The dynamic effect on the crowds continued:

> The apostles performed many miraculous signs and wonders among the people. And all the believers used to meet together in Solomon's Colonnade. No one else dared join them, even though they were highly regarded by the people. Nevertheless, more and more men and women believed in the Lord and were added to their number. As a result, people brought the sick into the streets and laid them on beds and mats so that at least Peter's shadow might fall on some of them as he passed by. Crowds gathered also from the towns around Jerusalem, bringing their sick and those tormented by evil spirits, and all of them were healed.
>
> Acts 5:12–16

People continued to be converted: "So the word of God spread. The number of disciples in Jerusalem increased rapidly, and a large number of priests became obedient to the faith" (Acts 6:7). As we go on in the book of Acts the same pattern continues. When Paul and Barnabas went to Iconium, "they spoke so effectively that a great number of Jews and Gentiles believed" (Acts 14:1). They spent a considerable time there "speaking boldly for the Lord, who confirmed the message of his grace by enabling them to do miraculous signs and wonders" (Acts 14:3). In Lystra a crippled man was healed (Acts 14:8). In Derbe "they preached the good news in that city and won a large number of disciples" (Acts 14:21).

Later on, Luke tells us what happened to twelve Ephesian men: "When Paul placed his hands on them, the Holy Spirit came on them, and they spoke in tongues and prophesied" (Acts 19:6). Further, in Ephesus, "God did extraordinary miracles through Paul, so that even handkerchiefs and aprons that had touched him were taken to the sick, and their illnesses were cured and the evil spirits left them" (Acts 19:11–12).

Far from dwindling away through the period covered by the book of Acts, this spiritual dynamic continued. Even in the last chapter we read of Paul praying for Publius' father: "His father was sick in bed, suffering from fever and dysentery. Paul went in to see him and, after prayer, placed his hands on him and healed him. When this had happened, the rest of the sick on the island came and were cured" (Acts 28:8–9). All the way through we see the dynamic effect of the coming of the kingdom of God accompanied by conversions, miraculous signs, healings, visions, tongues, prophecy, raising the dead, and casting out evil spirits. The same God is at work today among us. Evangelism can still be dynamic and effective.

Effective evangelism requires the filling and refilling of the Spirit

I'm not referring here to a "second blessing;" what I am talking about is experiencing God as Trinity: Father, Son, and Holy Spirit. This is an ongoing experience. Jesus told His disciples, "You will receive power when the Holy Spirit comes on you; and you will be my witnesses in Jerusalem, and in all Judea and Samaria, and to the ends of the earth" (Acts 1:8). On the day of Pentecost the promise of Jesus was fulfilled and "all of them were filled with the Holy Spirit and began to speak in other tongues as the Spirit enabled them" (Acts 2:4).

However, it did not end there. Later on we read of Peter being "filled with the Spirit" again (Acts 4:8). Still later the disciples (including Peter) were filled again (Acts 4:31). The filling of the Holy Spirit is not a one-off experience. Paul urges the Christians of Ephesus "to be filled with the Spirit" (Ephesians 5:18) and the emphasis is on continuing to be filled. Professor Wayne Grudem writes the most useful chapter I know of on this subject in his masterful *Systematic Theology*.[14]

As we look at the great evangelists of more recent history we see how many speak of such experiences. St. Philip Neri, living in sixteenth-century Rome, at the age of twenty-nine, experienced an extraordinary visitation from God's Spirit on the night before Pentecost 1544. As he was absorbed in prayer, he saw a ball of fire enter his mouth and travel down to his heart. The sensation of intense heat—that all-consuming fire of God's love—was so great that he threw himself on the ground to cool himself, pleading, "Oh, enough Lord, enough. I can't take any more." Filled with compassion, he began to spend time on the streets of Rome, looking for opportunities to share the gospel and pray for the sick, many of whom were miraculously healed. St. Philip brought the joy of the Lord to an entire city. He was a priest who, by following the Spirit's prompting, spawned a revival.

John Wesley (1703–1791), the founder of modern Methodism, wrote of an occurrence on New Year's Day 1739:

> About three in the morning, as we were continuing instant in prayer, the power of God came mightily upon us . . . many cried out for exceeding joy, and many fell to the ground. As soon as we recovered a little from that awe and amazement at the presence of His Majesty, we broke out with one voice, We praise thee, O God, . . . [15]

The result was that "the Holy Spirit began to move among us with amazing power when we met in his name." When anyone fell down under the power, they were prayed for until they were "filled with the peace and joy of the Holy Spirit," which was frequently "received in a moment." Wesley's journal is full of such accounts. One Quaker, who objected to such goings on, "went down as thunderstruck" and rose to cry aloud: "Now I know you are a prophet of the Lord."

Wesley concluded: "Similar experiences continued to increase as I preached. It seemed prudent to preach and write on the work of the Holy Spirit."[16] He preached regularly at Bristol's Newgate prison where the jailer, Abel Dagge, had been converted under Whitefield in 1737:

> One Thursday Wesley preached on the text "He that believeth hath everlasting life" and at the end he prayed "If this is thy truth, do not delay to confirm it by signs following." Immediately "the power of God fell among us. One, and another, and another, sank to the earth . . . dropping on all sides as thunderstruck." One, Ann Davies, cried out. He went across and prayed over her and she began to praise God in joy.[17]

For thirty-five years George Whitefield (1714–1770) was the outstanding itinerant preacher in Britain and America and he changed the conventions of preaching, opening the way for mass evangelism. He wrote in his journal: "Was filled with the Holy Ghost. Oh, that all who deny the promise of the Father, might thus receive it themselves! Oh, that all were partakers of my joy!"[18]

Charles Grandison Finney (1792–1875) was one of history's greatest evangelists, considered by many to be the forerunner of modern evangelism. Finney's experience of the Holy Spirit occurred later on the same day as his conversion:

> The Holy Spirit descended upon me in a manner that seemed to go through me, body and soul. I could feel the impression, like a wave of electricity, going through and through me. Indeed, it seemed to come in waves and waves of liquid love; for I could not express it in any other way. And yet it did not seem like water but rather the breath of God. I can recollect distinctly that it seemed to fan me, like immense wings: and it seemed to me, as these waves passed over me, that they literally moved my hair like a passing breeze. No words can express the wonderful love that was shed abroad in my heart. I wept aloud with joy and love; and I do not know but I should say, I literally bellowed out the unutterable gushings of my heart. These waves came over me, and over me, and over me, one after another, until I recollect I cried out, "I shall die if these waves continue to pass over me." I said, "Lord, I cannot bear any more;" yet I had no fear of death.[19]

Perhaps the greatest evangelist of the nineteenth century was D. L. Moody (1837–1899). Early on in his ministry he was a successful superintendent of a Sunday school mission in Chicago. However, two old ladies in his congregation informed him after a service that they were praying for him because he lacked the power of the Spirit. Although he was annoyed at their suggestion, the more he pondered about it the more he knew they were right. He wrote later that

> There came a great hunger into my soul. I did not know what it was. I began to cry out as I never did before. I really felt that I did not want to live if I could not have this power for service . . . I was crying all the time that God would fill me with His Holy Spirit.

About six months later, as he was walking down Wall Street in New York City, the Holy Spirit came upon him powerfully. He wrote later:

> Oh! What a day, I cannot describe it! I seldom refer to it, it is almost too sacred an experience to name . . . I can only say that God revealed Himself to me, and I had such an experience of His love that I had to ask Him to stay His hand.

John Pollock, his biographer, adds that Moody needed never thirst again. "The dead, dry days were gone. 'I was all the time tugging and carrying water. But now I have a river that carries me.' "[20]

Moody's successor at his Bible Institute was the great American evangelist of the early 1900s, R. A. Torrey (1856–1928). In his book *The Baptism with the Holy Spirit* he wrote:

> It was a great turning point in my ministry when, after much thought and study and meditation, I became satisfied that the baptism with the Holy Spirit was an experience for today and for me, and set myself to obtain it. Such blessing came to me personally that I began giving Bible readings on the subject, and I have continued to do so with increasing frequency as the years have passed . . . It has been the author's unspeakable privilege to pray with many ministers and Christian workers for this great blessing, and after to learn from them or from others of the new power that had come into their service, none other than the power of the Holy Spirit.[21]

In his foreword to R. A. Torrey's book, *Why God Used D. L. Moody* Will H. Houghton wrote:

> Some of our readers may take exception to Dr. Torrey's use of the term, "the baptism with the Holy Ghost." Perhaps if Dr. Torrey lived in our day and saw some of the wild fire in connection with that expression, he would use some other phrase. But let no one quibble about an experience as important as the filling with the Spirit. In this little book, Dr. Torrey quotes Mr. Moody as saying, in a discussion on this very matter, "Oh, why will they split hairs? Why don't they see that this is just the one thing that they themselves need? They are good teachers, they are wonderful teachers, and I am so glad to have them here, but why will they not see that the baptism of the Holy Ghost is just the one touch that they themselves need?"[22]

I think that there can be little doubt that the greatest evangelist of last century was Billy Graham (b. 1918). In his authorized biography, John Pollock tells how Billy Graham visited Hildenborough Hall and heard Stephen Olford speak on the subject "Be not drunk—but be filled with the Spirit." Billy Graham asked to see Olford privately and Olford expounded the fullness of the Holy Spirit in the life of a believer. "At the close of the second day they prayed, 'like Jacob of old laying hold of God,' " recalls Olford, "crying, 'Lord, I will not let Thee go except Thou bless me', until we came to a place of rest and praising;" and Graham said, "This is a turning-point in my life. This will revolutionize my ministry."[23]

In 1977, Raniero Cantalamessa, preacher to the Papal Household and Franciscan Professor of Theology, prayed to be filled with the Spirit. He had a vision of the cross:

> I was convinced at that moment that this renewal goes straight to the heart of the gospel, which is the cross of Jesus Christ!
> . . . Somebody said: "You will experience a new joy in proclaiming my word" . . . I can tell you this prophecy has come true. I have experienced a new joy in proclaiming the Word of God . . . the Scriptures came alive . . . The love of Scripture which results from the Holy Spirit is unbelievable . . . I realized that I had a new desire for prayer . . . When the Spirit comes, he says: "Abba, Abba."
> . . . One day as I was praying in my cell in the friary, I prayed for the first time in a manner vaguely like speaking in tongues; not exactly the same, but somewhat similar. For a moment there was a very deep-down communication—nothing verbal or visible—but I sensed that Jesus was passing in front of me.[24]

One of the keys to Alpha is having a team of Spirit-filled people using every gift they possess to lead others to Christ. "Evangelization will never be possible without the action of the Holy Spirit," concluded Pope Paul VI. Those who come to Christ on the course know that a radical change has occurred in their lives because they have been filled with the Holy Spirit. This experience of God gives them the stimulus and power to invite their friends to the next Alpha course.

In the rest of this book I want to look at the practical outworking of this vision and intersperse it with stories of some of those whose lives have been changed by attending an Alpha course.

THE STORY OF
NIGEL SKELSEY

CHAPTER 2

NIGEL SKELSEY

Nigel Skelsey rose quickly to the position of picture editor of a national newspaper, but felt he had lost his soul in the process. He joined an Alpha course at Holy Trinity Brompton and subsequently wrote a letter about the effect it had had on his life. With his permission, the letter is reproduced here.

Dear Nicky,

I was going to start this letter by saying, "Just a short note to tell you what the Alpha weekend meant to me," but I'm afraid it's turned into a long note. Please bear with me, but it's something I feel I need to get down on paper.

In 1979 my father died of stomach cancer and it was at that time that my Christian faith went on the back burner, and for the last fifteen years I haven't known why. It wasn't, as one might suppose, the question of suffering and a loving God. That wasn't a problem for me. I have subsequently found out it was far more deep-rooted than a moral dilemma.

For most of my life I have felt I've been a huge disappointment both to God and my parents. When I left school I spent three years at theological college training to be a church minister with a genuine desire to be an evangelist, but I failed academically, ending up with the double burden of not only being looked upon by my parents as a failure but also, I felt, by God as well.

I decided to pursue a career in photography, which was a hobby of my father's, with the hope of winning my parents' approval, and I joined a publishing company as a tea boy on a newly-launched photographic magazine. I had been there six months when my father got ill and eventually died. Just two weeks after his death the staff, on what was an ailing magazine, were laid off or left of their own volition. The tea boy was the only one left and was promptly made editor by default. It was success of sorts and something of which my father would have been incredibly proud. But he wasn't there to see it and I was devastated.

For the next fifteen years there followed a faithless and obsessive pursuit of success for its own sake. Every time I achieved something I would knock it on the head and start again from scratch. I was like a child with building bricks. I would build a tower and shout, "Look, Dad!" before knocking it down and building another one to impress him with.

My career was like a roller coaster. The ailing magazine, more by luck than judgment, given my inexperience, was turned round and within two years was the biggest selling monthly photographic magazine in the country. At the height of its success, and after only two years in the job, I left to join another magazine, which was in a poor state. Within two years circulation was surging to the point of overtaking the first magazine. Once more success came quickly, but it wasn't enough and after another two years I put an end to that and decided to launch my own photographic magazine, which, within no time at all, became renowned around the world, picking up publishing awards along the way.

Another two years had gone by and I still wasn't satisfied, so in 1987 I decided that I wanted to be picture editor of a national newspaper. I had no experience in that particular industry and to all, except the totally demented, it did not enter the realms of possibility. Since I was fast joining the ranks of the totally demented I didn't see the problem and within three years, at thirty-seven, I became the picture editor of the *Sunday Telegraph*.

Just before Christmas 1993 I turned forty and, probably like many on reaching that age, decided to reflect on what I had achieved and possibly where the next challenge lay. Forgetting the spiritual side, which was non-existent anyway, I was very satisfied. I had everything I had ever wanted in life: a fulfilling, well-paid job, a beautiful wife, two great sons, and a Porsche 911 on the drive. But at what cost?

I discovered that my nickname at the *Telegraph* was "The Beast."

Despite the affectionate undertones that many nicknames have, it told
me something about myself that I didn't like. I also overheard someone
else say that I was not truly happy unless I was at war with someone.
They were right. In fact, if conflict didn't happen to come my way then
I created it. Life had become a great battlefield.

Jesus said, "Love your neighbor as yourself," but my trouble was
that deep down I hated myself and I hated my neighbor as myself. My
motto was: "Forget revenge, get your retaliation in first!" I was like
some aging prizefighter who doesn't know when to give up. Every
single day of the last fifteen years has been a brawl, only, unlike a
boxing match, the bell never came at the end of each round. Worst of
all I looked in the bathroom mirror one morning and saw reflected
back someone I just didn't know any more. Over the next few days
the words of Jesus kept coming back to me, "What good will it be
for a man if he gains the whole world, yet forfeits his soul?", and I
realized that I had done just that. In my own little world I literally had
everything I ever wanted but I had lost my soul in the process.

Then on New Year's Day a friend whom I hadn't seen for years came
for dinner. What struck me was that he wasn't the person I used to
know. Even though a Christian, my old friend was the most dreadful
pessimist, whereas the new version sitting in front of me was full of
vigor, optimism and genuine happiness. And he started to tell me
about the great work that the Holy Spirit had done in his life. He went
on to describe how he had felt a failure all his life and how his father
had been hugely disappointed in him and, without warning, I burst
into inconsolable floods of tears at the dinner table: something The
Beast was not prone to doing!

He was describing what was locked away deep in my subconscious
and, although I didn't realize it, had been dominating my life all these
years. Unrattled, he stood up and prayed over me and I felt the most
extraordinary tingling sensation flooding through me, flushing out
all the deep-rooted unhappiness that had slowly festered beneath the
surface over the years.

I had experienced something I didn't understand, but which had a
profound effect on me. I woke up the next morning like a man obsessed
with a new ambition. I sensed God loved me and that I wasn't written
off in His eyes. I was still heavily chained at the bottom of a deep, dark

prison, only someone had banged a hole in the wall and a chink of light was spilling in, giving me a taste of the freedom that was there if only I could grasp hold of it.

In the summer I had been on holiday in Switzerland and had read an article in a magazine I found about the Alpha course at Holy Trinity Brompton. The one thing that had stuck in my mind was how the work of the Holy Spirit was described as being of paramount importance. I knew in my heart I had to have this power in my life at any cost so I found out where the church was, enrolled on the course and focused on the weekend. I felt like a dying man waiting for a life-saving operation. Never mind the weeks of pre-med, I just had to get into the operating room.

The weekend I had been waiting for, like a child waiting for Christmas, finally arrived . . . and I didn't want to go! I didn't realize what a spiritual battle I was about to experience. I lay in bed at the conference center on the Friday night and went through an onslaught the like of which I have never experienced before and I hope I never do again. Voices screamed in my head to get out, go home, I was making a fool of myself, God wouldn't do anything for me, I was beyond hope, I was a failure and so on. I tried to pray but I couldn't. I just lay there for what seemed like hours and got the biggest mauling of my life.

I woke up in the morning, shattered. I looked at the order of play, saw that the third session (which I had identified as the main one) was at 4.30 pm and simply hung on like a marathon runner weaving his way up the final straight with nothing but the finishing tape as the focus of his attention.

I'll never forget that final session. I felt as though I was being torn in two. Halfway through I just couldn't stand it any more. The prize was so near but we were getting there so slowly! I literally wanted to scream out, "Do it now! Do it now! I can't hold out any longer." I'm not exaggerating when I say I was in agony. Then God came, and oh, the relief.

Do you know, for the first time in my life I feel normal. It seems a strange thing to say but it keeps hitting me just how normal I feel! I also feel loved. I am accepted for who I am and I feel free. Terribly clichéd, isn't it? But I feel so free!

Yesterday I read some words of Paul in Philippians that express so deeply how I now feel about my "achievements" of the last fifteen years: "But whatever was to my profit I now consider loss for the sake of Christ. What is more, I consider everything a loss compared to the surpassing greatness of knowing Christ Jesus my Lord, for whose sake I have lost all things. I consider them rubbish, that I may gain Christ and be found in him . . . But one thing I do: Forgetting what is behind and straining toward what is ahead, I press on towards the goal to win the prize for which God has called me heavenward in Christ Jesus" (Philippians 3:7–9, 13–14).

I don't know what the future holds or where and how God will lead me; at the moment I'm just enjoying a honeymoon period! Which brings me to the point of this letter. Thank you for helping to bring to completion what was started on New Year's Day.

Regards,

Nigel

Nigel Skelsey now works for Alpha International, where he is developing an initiative for those battling addictions, called
The Recovery Course.

CHAPTER 3

THE STRUCTURE OF ALPHA

The ALPHA mnemonic

A is for anyone

That is, anyone interested in finding out more about the Christian faith. This includes at least five categories of people.

1. *Those who are not Christians.* Alpha is an evangelistic course, designed primarily for people who would not call themselves Christians. In the U.K., while 72 percent of the population would label themselves as Christians, 63 percent of the population would also describe themselves as nonreligious.

2. *Those who are not churchgoers.* In the U.K., 62 percent of the population never attend any form of church service. These are the people we aim to attract. There is a very big pool in which to fish.

The excitement of Alpha is seeing people outside the church coming to faith in Christ, being filled with the Holy Spirit, getting excited about Jesus, and going out and telling their friends. The buzz and excitement come from seeing people's lives being changed by the power of God.

Alpha has a totally different feel when we get people from categories one and two on the course. I have never experienced this myself, but I am told that if it is only Christians on the course, it can all become a bit negative. Sometimes the course ends up as a theological nit-picking discussion. It can all go slightly downhill, in a rather unhelpful way. All you need is one unchurched person, for example Fred, who is not a Christian, and then all the Christians behave themselves! Instead of wondering what is wrong with the talk theologically, they are all praying, "Lord, I do hope that Fred understands that." When Fred comes to faith in Christ, and as a result goes back to his wife and his family is reunited, there is such joy and excitement that Fred brings his friends on the next course, and so on.

3. *Those who are new Christians.* Alpha also works well with people who are new Christians. It ties in very well with other types of evangelism such as mass evangelism or personal evangelism. If someone has just come to faith in Christ through some other means, Alpha is a great place for them to put down the foundations of their Christian faith.

4. *Those who want to brush up on the basics.* There may be some people who have been going to church all their lives but feel they have never really grasped the basics of the Christian faith, or never really experienced the love of God for themselves. I heard Bob Buford, an American businessman who co-founded Leadership Network, make an interesting point. He said, "For many people, going to church is like going to a movie that is halfway through. Nobody ever tells them what happened in the first half of the movie." Alpha is like the bridge that tells people what happened in the first half of the movie so that they can understand the rest of it.

5. *Those new to the church.* Many people are daunted by going to a new church. If it is a large church, they feel intimidated by the numbers and wonder how they can ever get to know anyone. If it is a small church, they might feel very visible and awkward, like a stranger walking into a family party. If they come on an Alpha course, by definition the vast majority of the people on the course are new to the church because they are new Christians, not Christians, or not churchgoers. They get to know a group of people who, like them, are new to the church; they make friends and that makes it much easier when they start coming to church. It also introduces them to the values of the church.

L is for learning and laughter
We believe it is possible to learn about the Christian faith and have a great deal of fun at the same time. There is always a lot of laughter over the meals and in discussion groups. During the talks we try to introduce as much humor as we can. Being British, it is mainly self-

deprecating humor! At the beginning of every evening, during the announcements, we always stand up and tell a joke.

Alpha has been running since 1977. Since then we have been collecting jokes. We now have a grand total of six jokes! We tell those six jokes over and over again. We are always very grateful to the hosts and helpers (who have heard those six jokes many times) and indeed the guests who laugh out of all proportion to the joke's merits or the joke-teller's ability.

Humor breaks down barriers and makes people feel relaxed. We are trying to avoid intensity, because intensity is very off-putting to people outside the church. G. K. Chesterton wrote, in his book *Orthodoxy*:

One settles down into a sort of selfish seriousness; but one has to rise to a gay self-forgetfulness [to use an old fashioned sense of the word] . . . Seriousness is not a virtue . . . It is really a natural trend or lapse into taking oneself gravely because it is the easiest thing to do. It is much easier to write a good *Times* leading article than a good joke in *Punch*. Solemnity flows out of [people] naturally; but laughter is a leap. It is easy to be heavy: hard to be light.[1]

P is for pasta or potatoes or paella or pizza

Pasta is not a theological term, although in a sense it is. Someone said to me, "There is something almost sacramental about the meal on Alpha." As Robert Jenson wrote, "All meals are intrinsically religious occasions, indeed sacrifices, and were so understood especially in Israel

… sharing a meal is therefore always a communal act of worship and establishes fellowship precisely before the Lord."[2] The meal on Alpha has a profound significance because it is over the meal that friendships are formed.

H is for helping one another

It is amazing to watch a group of people from outside the church changing over the course of ten weeks. There are many factors involved. We would like to think that the key factors are our talks or the gifts of the hosts and helpers, but very often it is the guests themselves who are helping one another.

I think of a group I had—a typical Alpha group, none of whom were churchgoers. They were all negative for the first few weeks. There was a guy named Matthew. Matthew had been dragged along by his wife, who was not a Christian—in fact she was Jewish. But she was very interested in going on the Alpha course, and he had been to chapel at school but had not been to church since. So she dragged him along. And he was the most negative person. He was negative really until about week five.

Everybody else was being negative that night, and Matthew hadn't said anything. So I turned to Matthew and I said, "Matthew, what do you think?" He said, "Well, it happened to me." So I said, "What happened to you?" He said, "I shook on my bed in the middle of the night for three hours." The other people in the group thought this was the funniest thing they had ever heard—Matthew shaking on his bed for three hours in the middle of the night—they fell off their chairs they were laughing so hard.

When they had picked themselves up from the floor, they said, "What do you mean, you shook for three hours on your bed in the middle of the night?" He said, "Well, it's like this: the other night, I couldn't sleep. So I thought I'd try that prayer that you pray. I repented of my sins, I thanked Jesus for dying for me and I asked him to come and fill me with the Holy Spirit, and then I shook for three hours!"

The other people were on the edge of their seats! Within ten days every single person in that group had come to faith in Christ. I remember them on the Alpha weekend, arms around each other, praying for each other. Matthew had helped the others.

A is for ask anything

Alpha starts with an A and ends with an A. The final A stands for *ask anything*. No question is regarded as too simple. We find that older people are sometimes embarrassed by how simple their questions are. No question is too hostile. Some of the people who come on the course are very angry. That is fine. We want people who are angry, confused, or antagonistic to come—that is who the course is designed for.

A typical evening

Most courses run in the evening, but there are highly effective courses running during the daytime (see Appendices C and D). These run in different venues: churches, homes, schools, offices, prisons, nightclubs, and restaurants. The guests range from mothers with young children to university students, from city high-flyers to gangs living in projects, from police officers to prisoners. We have 160 prisons in the U.K.; 130 of those prisons are now running Alpha. Over 15,000 men and women have been through Alpha in prisons throughout the U.K., and it has now spread to eighty countries around the world.

Alpha can run at different times of day, but the most typical is the evening course.

6:30 P.M.	Hosts and helpers meet to pray
7:00 P.M.	Dinner
7:30 P.M.	Welcome
7:40 P.M.	Songs of worship
8:00 P.M.	Talk (see Appendix A for list of talks and suggested order)
8:50 P.M.	Coffee
9:00 P.M.	Small groups
9:30 P.M.	Finish

At 6:30 P.M. we meet to pray and prepare. The meeting of the hosts and helpers at the beginning of the evening for prayer and organization is of great importance. We have found that prayer is the key to everything that happens on Alpha. We encourage people to pray on their own; we

also have a prayer meeting early on a Tuesday morning and, critically, we get together to pray just before the guests arrive on the evening itself.

At this meeting it is helpful to run through the evening, focusing on the subject matter and considering helpful questions for the small groups. It is also a time to deal with administration, particularly for the Alpha Weekend and Celebration Dinner.

At 7:00 P.M. dinner is served. When Alpha was small (around twelve guests) each person on the course took a turn to cook dinner (starting with the hosts and helpers). As it grew, we reached a point where we had over ten small groups. Each small group then took turns cooking dinner. This system was totally restructured when we reached over 200 and had to employ a caterer and ask the guests for a small contribution to cover the costs. If they cannot afford to contribute, they are still welcome to have the meal.

Eating together is an essential part of the course, as it gives people the chance to get to know others in a relaxed way. Friendships grow over the course, especially within the small group, in an extraordinary way. We have found that it is better to use the meal time to talk to the guests about the things they are interested in: their work, their leisure, their hobbies, and sporting interests—anything, in fact, apart from religion!

At 7:30 P.M. we welcome everyone and give announcements. This time is used to recap what happened the previous week as well as to recommend any books and the recording of the previous week's talk, for those who may have missed it. One of the rules we have on Alpha is that there should be no general announcements for anything that is not directly related to the course. This can be off-putting for guests. Towards the end of the course, we also use this time to talk about the weekend and the dinner. Then we tell the all-important joke.

At 7:40 P.M. we have a short time of singing. We explain carefully what we are going to do. I often quote what the apostle Paul says in his letter to the Ephesians: "Speak to one another with psalms, hymns and spiritual songs. Sing and make music in your heart to the Lord" (Ephesians 5:19). We have a mixture of old and new. We always start the first night with a well-known hymn for the benefit of those who might find that more familiar. As the course goes on we tend towards more modern songs, changing gradually from singing about God to singing directly to Him, and we increase the length of time we spend in worship from about five minutes on the first night to about fifteen to twenty minutes towards the end of the course. We try not to move too quickly at the beginning and I explain that what matters is that we "sing and make music in our hearts." Some may not be ready to participate, and it is fine for them simply to listen until they are ready to join in.

The worship leader must sound confident, even if he or she is not. We have found that it is better that the worship leader gives no introduction to the songs. He or she is there to lead worship rather than to give what can easily become another talk.

Unless worship can be led and music played competently it is probably better not done at all. Some Alpha courses run without any singing. It is not an essential part of the course. The very small courses where guests listen to CDs or watch DVDs would not normally have any singing. However, people running a small or medium-sized course have found that it is enriching to play a worship CD as backing if they do not have a worship leader, and this approach also works well (see Appendix H).

I have found that although many find the singing the most difficult part of the course to begin with, and some are even hostile towards it, by the end they often find it is the part they value most. For many, such singing is their first experience of communicating with God. It also helps people to make the step from Alpha to the church, where the worship of God is central.

At 7:50 p.m., after the singing, we have the talk. This may be given by the course leader, or even a host or helper who has the appropriate gifts and the time to prepare the material. We have produced the whole course on DVD, which some people prefer to use. Some course leaders find it distances them from the material, and enables the guests to be more open and honest in their response to the talk! Others find that there is simply too much else to think about, and that time saved preparing talks enables them to organize the administration and pastoral care more effectively. They may go on to do the talks themselves at a later date.

In the long term, we would recommend a live speaker doing the talks, but the DVD provides an effective second best. It is useful if the guests follow the talks by using an *Alpha Course Manual*, although they should not be charged for these. It is very important that people should hear the gospel free of charge. On a large course it is necessary to have someone who is used to and gifted at speaking to more sizeable gatherings. This inevitably limits the number of speakers available.

An essential resource for live speakers is the book *Questions of Life*, which contains the content of the Alpha course. The best way to prepare a live talk is to read the relevant chapter —for example, "Who Is Jesus?"—and give the talk in your own words, using your own illustrations and applications that are relevant to the people who you are speaking to. There are also a number of resources available online at alphafriends.org to help you prepare a live talk.

(In the next few paragraphs, when referring to a chapter in the book *Questions of Life*,[3] which is based on the Alpha talks, I will use the abbreviation QoL followed by the chapter number.)

The first week the talk is on "Who Is Jesus?" (QoL 2). In weeks two to six we cover the material in chapters 3–7. At this point we often have a weekend away. If we do, then the talk on week seven is, "How Can I Resist Evil?" (QoL 11). If the weekend away is at any other time, "How Can I Resist Evil?" would follow it. This is because I have found that the talk about spiritual warfare only becomes really relevant after people have experienced the power of the Holy Spirit.

On week eight we look at "Why and How Should We Tell Others?" (QoL 12). At this stage, I start to talk about the Celebration Dinner at the end of the course. The following week we look at the subject of healing (QoL 13). This session is typically followed by prayer in small groups, or a corporate time of ministry for smaller courses (see Chapter 13 in this book for "Prayer Ministry on Alpha" guidelines).

On the final night we look at the subject of the church (QoL 14). The main aim of this talk is to start integrating those who have been on Alpha into the life of the church. We explain how the home group system in the church works and encourage them to join such a group. Often the whole small group on Alpha will join the same home group.

Each week, at the end of the talk, we go into small groups (see Chapter 9 in this book) and aim to finish at 9:30 P.M. It is tempting to run over time if the discussion is going well, but it is generally a bad idea. If the evening ends in the middle of a lively debate, the group tends to feel motivated to return next week. Conversely, if the group ends late, it becomes a reason to drop out after a long day at work.

The Alpha weekend

The weekend away is a crucial part of the course. This is the time that we devote to teaching on the work of the Holy Spirit in the individual lives of those on the course. The material covered is in chapters 8, 9, 10, and 15 of *Questions of Life*. It is possible to cover this material in a single day. Sometimes we have a Saturday locally for those who cannot make one of the weekends. However, there are enormous advantages to the weekend away.

We have found that friendships are formed on a weekend much more easily than on a single day. As people travel together, have meals together, go for walks, enjoy the evening entertainments, and receive Holy Communion together on Sunday morning, there is a cementing of the friendships that have begun to form in the early weeks. In this relaxed environment people start to unwind and some of the barriers begin to come down. I have found that many make as much progress spiritually during the weekend away as in the rest of the course put together.

I know that it is hard to find a venue, but it is usually possible if plans are made far enough ahead. It may be worth joining with other churches in the area. If members of the congregation cannot afford to go away, then the weekend could take place in a local venue. However, in most congregations it is possible for those who can afford to pay to help those who cannot afford to pay anything at all or only a part. We always encourage people to attend the weekend whether they can afford to pay or not, as it is such a crucial element in the course, and we have always found that the financial arrangements resolve themselves. On the Sunday morning of the weekend, we have a collection, and assure people they are free to put in nothing, or as much or little as they would like. We then pray that God would be faithful to His promise to "supply all your needs according to his riches in Christ Jesus" (Philippians 4:19). We are amazed by God's faithfulness.

The timetable for our weekend is as follows:

Friday

6:30 P.M. onwards	Arrive
8:00–9:30 P.M.	Dinner
9:30 P.M.	Worship and a short introduction to the weekend—this can include a brief talk based on John 15 or perhaps a testimony.

Saturday

8:30 A.M.	Breakfast
9:00 A.M.	Hosts' and helpers' meeting
9:30 A.M.	Worship
	Talk 1 – "Who is the Holy Spirit?'"
10:45 A.M.	Coffee
11:15 A.M.	Talk 2 – "What Does the Holy Spirit Do?"
12:00 noon	Small group discussion. Often we look at 1 Corinthians 12:4–11 and the subject of spiritual gifts. It is vital to make time to talk about the gift of tongues during this small group discussion. People may be prompted by the passage to discuss their confusion and fears on the subject. Sometimes, one member of the group is able to share a positive experience, for example how the gift helped them to pray, or even just a real desire to experience the gift. Whatever people say, it is a good opportunity to get the subject in he open, and helps people feel much more comfortable when the gift of tongues is discussed on Saturday evening.
1:00 P.M.	Lunch
Free afternoon	Activities can be organized, e.g., sports, walks etc.
4:00 P.M.	Optional tea
5:00 P.M.	Worship
	Talk 3 – "How Can I be Filled with the Holy Spirit?"

7:00 P.M.	Dinner
8:30 P.M.	Entertainment. A variety of skits and songs without anything distasteful, religious, or nasty. We have found that the entertainment contributes to people's enjoyment of the weekend, but only if they realize participation is entirely voluntary! It is extraordinary to uncover hidden gifts, and many who contribute suddenly become more confident and more "part of things," and the course gains unity and momentum.

Sunday

9:00 A.M.	Breakfast
9:20 A.M.	Hosts' and helpers' meeting
9:45 A.M.	Small group discussion. An opportunity for each guest to talk about what they have seen and heard so far. The feel of the group will probably have changed: objective questions often give way to subjective experiences as people share their responses, and may start to open up at a new level.
10:30 A.M.	Worship Talk 4 – "How Can I Make the Most of the Rest of My Life?" Holy Communion
1:00 P.M.	Lunch
Free afternoon	Hopefully everybody meets again at the evening service at church

Sometimes people say, "We love Alpha! We think Alpha is fantastic! We love the idea of the meal, the discussion groups, the series of talks and so on. We love everything about Alpha —except the bit about the Holy Spirit. Could we run Alpha without the Holy Spirit?" Now, I know what they mean—they don't quite mean that. They mean without the weekend and the part about the person and the work of the Holy Spirit.

The answer is that it would not be Alpha. I often think it would be like a car that looks the same as any other car but is without an engine. One denomination did a survey of all the churches that were running Alpha, and they found there were a handful of churches where Alpha was not working. There were also a handful of churches that had cut out the weekend or the day on the Holy Spirit. They were the same churches.

Some people say, "Well, we wouldn't do that, but what we would like to do is take out the bit about speaking in tongues. Could we leave that out?"

When we first went to the United States to do a conference there, a church growth expert came to see me and said, "Look, if you cut out the bit about speaking in tongues, I could get Alpha running in all these denominations and streams . . . but you do need to cut that bit out." I wondered whether he was right. Perhaps that shouldn't be part of the course. We thought about it carefully. All the way through we had seen the providence of God and also we had seen the effect on our course of this subject's inclusion. We did not feel it was right to omit it.

About a year later we were doing a conference in Nashville, Tennessee. Right at the start of the conference a Pentecostal pastor from Columbus, Ohio, came up to talk to me. He was so excited. He said, "We have just run our first Alpha course. We didn't allow anyone to come unless they brought a friend from outside the church, and we had seventy-five people on the course." He told us amazing stories about what had happened.

I said, "Tell me: what did you find difficult as a Pentecostal running Alpha?" He replied, "Well, we found the ministry difficult." He was talking about the prayer ministry. I said, "Don't you have prayer ministry in the Pentecostal church?" He said, "Oh yes, we have prayer ministry in our church. But the style is very different. In our particular church when we have ministry we like lots of noise! We have a band, we have loud noise and we have lots of shouting!" He went on, "When you ask the Holy Spirit to come, you only ask Him quietly. We didn't think the Holy Spirit would come if we only asked Him quietly! But we decided to try it, and He came!"

I said, "Well, was there anything else you found difficult as a Pentecostal running Alpha?" He said, "Yes, tongues." I replied, "I am so sorry, I thought you said that you were a Pentecostal!" He said, "You don't have *enough* about the gift of tongues. It is only one third of one talk—one forty-fifth of the Alpha course. If you see Alpha as we do, as a two-year program of adult Christian education, it is only one two-hundred-and-forty-fifth of the two-year program! This is the only time that it is mentioned."

On Alpha we say that you can be a Christian and filled with the Spirit and not speak in tongues. We don't believe there is such a thing as "first-class Christians who speak in tongues and second-class Christians who don't." We say that it is not the most important gift—in fact Paul often put it at the bottom of the list of gifts. Sometimes, people ask why we mention it at all in that case. Our answer is because we believe that both in the New Testament and also in experience it is often the first of the more obviously supernatural gifts of the Spirit that people begin to experience. The gift of tongues is a beginners' gift. Alpha is a course for beginners.

This Pentecostal pastor then said, "You don't insist on the gift and you don't have enough material on it," but he added, "We were willing to 'bend in love' and run it the way you do." I remember thinking, "Isn't that amazing?"

There may be other parts of the worldwide church at the opposite end of the spectrum who say, "Well, we wouldn't have anything at all about it, but maybe we can just 'bend a little bit in love' and do it the way that you do." As a result all over the world there are Catholics, Protestants, and Pentecostals all running the same course. We believe that could only be the providence of God.

THE STORY OF
PAUL COWLEY

CHAPTER 4

PAUL COWLEY

As a young man, Paul Cowley ended up in prison and later, after a brief marriage, became estranged from his son. Here, Paul tells the remarkable story of how God changed his life and how, following prayer, he was reconciled with his son and his father whom he had not seen for many years.

I left home when I was fifteen because I was expelled from school and couldn't stand my parents' arguments. I moved into an empty house with a bunch of skinheads and soon afterwards, my father divorced my mother. When I asked him why he had left he said he had only stayed with her because I was there.

For the next five years I had a variety of jobs. I was a butcher, a milkman, and I worked in a bakery. For five years I just blasted around as a scooter boy. I was doing everything that you shouldn't do. I got myself a criminal record for petty stuff—basically for stealing cars and joyriding. I ended up in HMP Risley, juvenile delinquent center, for a short time.

When I was twenty I started to realize that my life was going downhill rapidly and that I needed to do something about it. I saw a billboard seeking volunteers to join the Army and I decided to join up. It was a bit touch and go as to whether I got in or not—mainly because of my criminal record—but they selected me and I went into the Royal Artillery, doing twenty-six weeks basic training at Woolwich in London. I enlisted for three years at first and extended this to nine years while I was training. It all just seemed to fit—I loved it and fit in right away. I was determined to succeed and loved the stability of Army life as well as the responsibility.

After my training, I was posted to Germany and asked my girlfriend to marry me. A year later, we had a little boy. We were living in Hohne in Germany, on the north-west side near the border with Russia, and I was happy throwing myself into my work and career. I got into everything and was hungry for promotion. I didn't care who I stepped on, who I hurt, or what I did. The only thing I wanted to do was to get out of being a non-ranker, which I did quite quickly. I got to Staff Sergeant in four and a half years, which is quite unknown in the Artillery. It usually takes about eight or nine years. I was quite ruthless in order to get there and during that time my relationship with my wife started to deteriorate. We weren't getting along very well and I took another posting to get a promotion, moving to Chester in England.

While we were in Chester my wife and I got divorced. Why? For lots of reasons, the main one being because it just wasn't working. It was mostly my fault because I was after other women. I didn't value my relationship with my wife. I was more interested in other things. My son was three then. I didn't take my commitment to my wife or to my son seriously. Life was about me and wanting promotion and adventure.

I pursued my career in the Army as a single man but not for long. I soon met a woman, fell in love and married her quickly. The marriage didn't last long—just over a year and we were soon divorced.

I quickly got involved in Adventurous Training and it took me all over the place: Canada, Germany, Gibraltar. I was an instructor in mountain climbing, skiing, canoeing and white water rafting, and would take expeditions all over the place.

The years went by and I saw my son whenever I could fit him in. Occasionally, I would arrange for him to fly out to wherever I was so that we could have a weekend or a week together. I had a variety of different relationships with women through that time, so he would come out and meet them. Every time I saw him it would be great, but when I left he would break down and cry. He wanted to be with me, but I couldn't cope with that.

All this drove me crazy. I couldn't deal with the emotional or physical stress. If I was back in England we would sometimes have a few days together between my flights, but he was never a priority. I visited my mother and father when I was in England, but I didn't tell my father that I had seen my mother, because he would get really angry. When I saw my mom, I didn't mention my dad either. This deception all added to me feeling stressed. So I decided to escape, as I always did. This time I took a posting in Cyprus to teach climbing. They wanted someone to go out there for two or three weeks, but I extended it to ten weeks.

In August 1985, I was teaching junior soldiers to climb in a big ravine on the mountain area of Mount Troodos when we heard voices at the bottom. My climbing partner said, "There are girls down there."

I said, "I don't think so. Not around here. Only sheep and trees!"

We rappelled down a bit further and at the bottom were two girls sitting on a rock, doing some painting. We got talking and found out that they were named Amanda and Kristina and that they were art students travelling around the island drawing the countryside. They were on an exchange visit with an art college in Cyprus for six weeks. I invited them back to the camp. I wanted to be friends with both of them, but I ended up falling in love with Amanda.

When I got back to England I went to see her in London. We were both quite marriage-phobic, because of the breakdown of relationships in both our families. Her parents were divorced too, so the idea of marriage wasn't even a consideration. We ended up living together in Warwickshire—again because of a posting I had taken working with the Junior Leaders Regiment Royal Artillery who were stationed in Nuneaton.

During that time, my mother wanted to move to be near us but she became ill with cancer. Not long afterwards she died. It was quite a blow really because I was just getting a relationship back with her. I was really angry, but Amanda was amazing. She guided me and took control. It was a really difficult time for me.

While we were sorting through my mom's stuff, I found a Bible—the Good News Bible. I looked inside it and there were lots of passages marked. There was also a name and telephone number. We called the number and spoke to a lady who turned out to be a friend of my mother's from Manchester. She told me that my mother had become a Christian about two years ago and that she used to go to church and was just getting into a fellowship group when she left to live with us. My mom had never said anything about it to me. She had kept it quite secret. That blew my socks off really, because my mom was a hard northern woman and quite volatile. I couldn't take in the idea of her being a Christian.

My dad didn't want to come to Mom's funeral at first because they hadn't seen each other for a long time. They were very much in love with each other, but it was a sort of "Burton and Taylor" type marriage—incredibly intense—and they were both very angry with each other. I said it would be very special if he would come up to the funeral, which he finally did, but it was very difficult for him. He got lost trying to find the cemetery and he was late. We were just putting mom into the earth when he showed up. He was really stressed about that.

Then we went back home, across the road to the house, and we tried to talk about things. I realize now that he couldn't take the emotion of Mom being dead. He tried to talk to me about all the guilt he felt, but he just got upset. He got into his car and took off back to Manchester. After that, we had a falling out about some money and some possessions of my mom's that he wanted. My mom had left everything to me because I was the only relative she had. I took him around her house about a month later and said, "Dad, take what you want from the house. Whatever you want is yours. It is your furniture anyway." He got a bit angry about things and he was confused and mixed up. After that, I didn't see him for a few years.

Occasionally my son would come and stay with us. He has always gotten along well with Amanda but gradually he stopped coming and we lost contact. I have to admit that Amanda was a far greater priority to me than he was at that time.

After thirteen and a half years in the Army I had done five tours of Northern Ireland and one tour of the Falklands. I was not happy with the next posting that the Army offered me, so I left. I got headhunted for the position of Fitness Director at a men's health club in Mayfair. During that time Amanda really encouraged me to write to my father and to my son, which I found really difficult because I never got any replies. She said, "You need to keep writing. You need to keep that channel open." So I would write. When I felt melancholy, perhaps after looking at some photos of my mom, I would read her Good News Bible, but didn't really understand what I was reading.

Soon after this, Amanda and I were visiting some friends in Rye on the south coast for the weekend. On the Sunday morning we went for a walk along the seafront and I suddenly said to her, "I want to go to church."

Amanda nearly fell over and said, "What do you mean you want to go to church?"

I said, "Well, I just feel that I would like to go to church."

"You're probably going to be really bored," she said. But I went anyway and she was right, I was really bored. Some churches I went to must have had about ten people there—a vicar and a cat at the most.

After that, for the next few Sundays, I went to a variety of churches; I would sit at the back and listen. I was compelled to do it. I got very bored, but I still kept going.

Then Amanda's brother suggested that we go to Holy Trinity Brompton. We walked into HTB one Sunday in 1992 and the Reverend Tom Gillum was preaching. At the end of it he said, "If there is anyone here who is new to the church and would like to pray about whether this is the church for them, do come to the front and we'll get someone from the ministry team to pray for you."

So I said, "We might as well try this prayer stuff, Amanda. Let's go see."

We went forward and found ourselves talking to Tom Gillum. We told him what we were doing and how we were looking for a church. He prayed a very simple prayer, which I will never forget. He just put his hands on me and Amanda and he said, "Lord, I ask that You find these people a church. If it is this church then that will be fantastic, but if it isn't, Lord, I ask that You will plant them in an area where they will grow and develop their relationship with You."

I thought that was kind of a nice prayer. There was no pressure at all. He just said goodbye to us and hoped that he might see us again. I liked that, so I went back to the church. Then someone suggested the Alpha course and I thought, "If I was trying to be a mechanic I would go to maintenance classes." This seemed to be a course for people who wanted to find out about God.

So I read the literature and we attended the course. We were put in a group with a guy named Geoff Wilmot and I am sure I was Geoff's nightmare. I must have asked every question. Amanda told me to be quiet on lots of occasions, but I knew nothing and I wanted to know everything. I wanted the whole 2,000 years of Christianity explained to me! He was great—so patient.

After that, we were asked to come back to help on the next course, so we did. Before the end of the second course, I stopped thinking about the "head" stuff and concentrated more on putting it in my heart. I remembered reading in the Bible where Jesus says that we have to come to him as a child (Matthew 18:1–6). I thought, *What does that mean: "a child?"* I thought about my son and how he would always trust me. So I thought, *I am going to come to Him as a child,* and I gave my life to Christ. I gave him my heart and I committed myself to him. Amanda, who had done something similar at the age of thirteen but had never followed it through, did the same a little bit later.

As soon as I allowed God to "get me," my whole concept of life completely changed. It was like the scales were removed from my eyes. I had a different perspective on life completely. I started to reconsider my relationship with Amanda, because we weren't married. I began to think, *We should be married. What is this? We are sleeping together. We are living together. What is going on?* I just wasn't comfortable with it. One day when Amanda and I were in a coffee shop in West Hampstead, I pushed a little box towards her. She opened it and said, "What do you want?"

"I think we should get engaged," I said.

She replied, "I might not want to get engaged."

I said, "What do you mean you don't want to get engaged? I was going to ask you to marry me."

She answered, "Well, I don't want to marry you."

So my whole world started to fall apart. I thought, *What is going on? What do you mean you don't want to marry me? You have got to marry me. We are Christians. We have got to do this stuff.*

After eight years of a great relationship, we went back to the apartment and broke up. We had an almighty argument and she left me. She went to stay with Kristina, the girl she had been to Cyprus with. I remember sitting that night in the apartment with a bottle of wine on my own thinking, *Great! This is a good plan Lord! I am now crying. I am on my own. I am drinking and what is going on? I am doing what you tell me to do. I have asked her to marry me and she has left me and we have had a big argument.*

Through that night I was in a right state and, although I didn't know it at the time, Amanda was too. I called her up the next morning and I said, "Look, we need to talk."

We met at the Natural History Museum in London. We both took the day off work and sat for five hours talking about stuff that we had to work out. In the end we got back together.

We got married in Leicestershire, in a little village called Sheepy Magna. The day after our wedding, we got baptised in a river behind the church. It was freezing. After our honeymoon, we got involved with running an Alpha group with Geraldine and Russell Garner. They have been an amazing influence on both our lives, especially mine. After Alpha, we joined their home group, which was brilliant.

I started sharing stuff about my life and about Amanda's life. One night, after everyone had gone and it was just me and Amanda left, Geraldine said, "Do you want to pray about anything? You are always praying for people and you never get prayed for yourself."

I said, "No, I'm fine. We don't need anything."

Geraldine said, "Well, what about your son and your father?"

I replied, "No, they are fine. They are okay."

I realize now that there were two issues in my life at that time that I didn't want anyone to touch, because I had killed them off and they were gone—separate. She said, "Well, I think we should pray about it."

She prayed for reconciliation with my son and reconciliation with my father. I was very cynical and I said, "You're going to need a lot of help with that one!"

I sent a letter to my son and father explaining what had happened, who Jesus was, what He had done for me, how He had changed me and that my whole outlook on life was different. Still no replies.

Meanwhile, my son was having a hard time. He had been expelled from school for drugs (which I didn't know about) and was heavily involved in the rave scene. His relationship with his mother and his stepfather was deteriorating. He was now sixteen and his mother couldn't cope with his outbursts of anger, his not coming home, his staying out for days, and his drinking. In the end, she said, "I can't cope with you any more. I want you out of this house."

He went on to a party and after doing a heavy session of drugs, he left and went for a walk. He ended up running in a field. He said he ran and ran and ran, and then sat down under a tree and cried. He intended to kill himself. Then he cried out to God and said, "If there is anybody out there, then you had better come and help me." He slept in the field.

The next morning he went home to his mom and she said, "I think you need to speak to your father because you are just like he was." That was when he called me up.

So I got a phone call in my office out of the blue, "I want to come and see you, Dad."

"Okay, when?" I said.

"Today."

"When today?"

He said, "I'll be at King's Cross at seven o'clock."

I had not seen him or spoken to him for six years.

It was a Tuesday night—the night of our home group (by then we were running one of our own), so I told Amanda that I was going to need a lot of prayer cover for this. She got the whole group praying for this meeting at seven o'clock.

I went to King's Cross and saw him walking towards me. I had left a little cute boy but now this "thug" was walking towards me. He had dark glasses on and a small suitcase. It frightened the life out of me.

It was quite hard at first to talk. We went out that night for something to eat, just the two of us. I took him home and he started to share our life there. We talked and we talked and we talked. We talked about his life. We talked about the suicide attempt. We talked about Jesus. We just talked about all sorts of things.

I managed to get him a job through a contact that I had, so he started work there. It put him in a suit, which meant he had to tidy himself up.

I was praying for him to go to Alpha, but I didn't want to push it. In the end, one day as we were getting ready to go to a Sunday service, he said, "Oh, I'll come with you."

That was in January 1996. He came and he sat in church. Then he came again. He went from the hard aggressive stance, to the lighter stance, to standing up, to singing. Then he said, "I might do the Alpha course, Dad."

I said, "Okay, that would be great." I was singing and dancing under my breath!

One night at home half way through the course he said, "I want you to talk to me a bit more about Jesus and all that stuff." So Amanda and I did. In the end we prayed together on the settee and he gave his life to Christ then and there, which was amazing. Then his life started to change. He started to pray for things and his drugs are now out the window and he has stopped smoking.

Later that same week, I got a phone call from my dad saying that he wanted to see me. We had a strained phone call, but it was a start. A little later, my father came to London to see us. My father and son had quite a tearful reunion. They hadn't seen each other for nearly ten years. Dad even came to a service at Holy Trinity with us all and met our friends. After that, my son and I went to Macclesfield and spent a whole weekend with my dad. It is amazing to see how God reunited me with my son and my dad. Only the power of Jesus could do such a thing.

My dad passed away in 2003. Although he found it hard to talk about things we managed to have a better relationship. When I got ordained he said he was proud of me and I was able to talk with him openly about my faith.

Paul Cowley was ordained in 2002 and is now on the staff of Alpha International, where he is the church's Executive Director of Social Transformation, which works nationally and internationally.

CHAPTER 5

THE ALPHA RECIPE

In my last year in university, my wife Pippa (who was just a friend at that time) was working as a professional cook in Belgium. When we had friends around and needed to cook food, I would often ask her for a recipe. We were students living on a fairly simple diet. We had cereal for breakfast and bread and cheese for lunch. We had a pint of milk delivered every day. We bought a loaf of bread and some cheese. When the bread reached a certain stage of staleness we would put it out on the window sill to dry out. One time we had accumulated a lot of milk in our fridge and quite a lot of bread had been accumulated on our window sill. We also had one egg and a little cheese. So I called Pippa and said, "Is there a recipe that involves eggs, cheese, bread and milk?" She said, "Yes, there is. Take twelve eggs, whisk them together, add a little bit of milk, then soak the bread in the mixture, put a little cheese on the top and place it in the oven and you will make a soufflé." I thought, *Great, sounds absolutely perfect! Well, it won't matter that our proportions are slightly different.* So I put in the one egg, the seven pints of milk, soaked the bread in the milk, put a little cheese on top and stuck it in the oven. It was absolutely disgusting. It was not edible!

The problem was that I hadn't quite followed the recipe. I think sometimes people do the same with Alpha. They think, "Oh, well, perhaps we will just change it around a bit and see what happens." If people do that, the problem is that they will never know whether Alpha would have worked if they had run it according to the recipe. We recommend that churches follow the recipe, at least the first few times that they run it. It might just be that there is a reason why you need those twelve eggs and only a small amount of milk, rather than the other way round. But you will never discover unless you try it.

We have been running the Alpha course since 1977—and we have made so many mistakes. As a result of all those mistakes, we have come up with "the Alpha recipe": the ingredients and methods that are most simple to use and have been tried and tested again and again. We would recommend following that recipe closely. So what is the recipe?

When?

First, the dates need to be fixed. The course takes eleven weeks (including the party at the end). Alpha at Holy Trinity Brompton takes place on Wednesday evenings (although there is also a daytime Alpha course—see Appendix C). It is of utmost importance, in order to maintain the momentum, to run *at least* three courses a year. If this happens, then a guest can attend an Alpha course, come to faith in Christ, be filled with the Spirit, get excited about Jesus, and ask their friends on the next course. Clearly there must be a next course to ask their friends to, so you do not want too big a gap between courses. We used to run four a year, but due to the size we have had to cut down to three. The best times are usually during the autumn (October to December), spring (January to April) and summer (May to July).

Because Alpha is a rolling program, and also because it takes a little bit of time to adjust to it, I really do not think we can know whether Alpha works for us until we have run it at least nine times! There are two reasons for this: when a church first starts Alpha, the guests tend to be church members and the courses are quite large. After a while, most of the church members have done the course and the size of the course falls correspondingly. It is only after three or four courses have been held that fringe members and nonchurchgoers start filtering into the course and numbers start to rise again. This is when Alpha *actually* starts. One pastor from Kansas City came to an Alpha conference in an Anglican church in Toronto and went home saying, "I am going to go back and run this course nine times, whether it works or whether it doesn't." On his first course he had twenty people and they were all Christians —he found this part extremely boring! He had twelve people on the next course, but none of them were Christians. Within two years the course had grown to 125.

Alpha is not a quick-fix solution to church growth. However, if we want a long-term way to see people coming into the church, then I don't know of a more effective way than Alpha. The key is keeping going because it takes a number of times to de-bug it, to get used to it, to work out how it works for our situation. The vicar from one of our church plants told me recently that the breakthrough happened on their thirty-sixth Alpha course—so we need to persist!

Where?

A venue needs to be found. The ideal venue is a home. At Holy Trinity we had considerable hesitations about moving from a home after many years because such an environment is nonthreatening for those who do not go to church. We only did so eventually because of the increasing size of the course. When the course outgrows the home, a venue with a welcoming atmosphere needs to be found.

How do we get people to come?

Fifteen ways to attract people to your Alpha course

Encouraging people outside the church to attend the Alpha course is a hurdle that many churches find difficult to cross. Most people attend the course because they have been invited personally by a friend or family member, yet there are many ways of reaching out into the wider community and encouraging people to attend.

1. Friends, family, and work colleagues of those who did a previous course. The main way a course will grow is by people who have attended Alpha telling their friends, family, and work colleagues about their experience and inviting them on a subsequent course. We have certainly found at HTB that around 70 percent of people on each Alpha course have come through personal recommendation or invitation. The more we run Alpha, the more this builds. Some of those who have just completed a course may ask their friends on the next course, but equally they may ask them in a year's time or even in three years' time. This underlines the importance of running Alpha as a rolling program.

One of the aims of the talk "Why and How Should I Tell Others?" (Week 8) is to motivate the guests from our current course to invite their friends to the Alpha celebration dinner and the next Alpha course.

2. Alpha celebration dinners. The purpose of the Alpha celebration dinner is both to celebrate the end of one Alpha course and to launch the next course. It provides an easy way for guests to invite friends, family, and work colleagues to come and hear the talk "Is There More to Life Than This?" in a friendly environment. As part of the Alpha Initiative, dinner invitations have been produced. People can use these to invite their friends.

We aim to create an environment that is relaxed and nonthreatening. It should have the feel of a celebration party. We put out tablecloths, flowers, candles, and have music (not worship songs) playing in the background.

A suggested timetable is as follows:

7:00 P.M.	Guests arrive
7:15 P.M.	Dinner
8:30 P.M.	Interviews
8:50 P.M.	Talk – "Is There More to Life Than This?"
9:25 P.M.	Coffee
9:30 P.M.	People start to leave

The testimonies are a very important part of the evening (see point 9 for more detail on these interviews).

We suggest that copies of *Why Jesus?*[1] and invitations to the next course are available on the tables during coffee or dessert and/or as they leave at the end of the evening. We do not ask people to sign up for the course that evening as we find people prefer to remain anonymous. I suggest that they come to the first night of Alpha, and assure them that if they don't want to come back, no one will call them up or send them junk mail. This takes the pressure off them. Most who come to the first night continue to come on their own accord.

3. Congregation contacts. On average, a church of 100 people will have 300 family contacts and any number of friends, colleagues, and acquaintances. Research shows that the church door is a big barrier for many people. However, a personal invitation to an Alpha course by someone they know can be very attractive. This is one of the reasons why it is so important for the parish priest, minister, pastor, elder (i.e., the person who is leading the church) to be proactively encouraging the congregation to bring their friends.

I have a friend named Wes Richards, who is the pastor of an independent church in Slough. They have been running Alpha for a number of years, very successfully. They have had about seventy people coming to their celebration dinners. The course has run very well. Eighteen months ago he decided that they were going to change direction in this sense. Alpha is now part of their DNA. They were going to make it a central plank in their evangelistic strategy and he was really going to push it. He encouraged the congregation to bring their friends. He preached about it. That September the numbers went up from seventy at the celebration dinner to seven hundred.

4. *Baptism candidates*. Most churches have a personal fringe, but they also have an institutional fringe—that is to say, people who relate to the church as an institution. For example, in many parts of the church there are couples who bring their children for baptism. We have found that Alpha is an ideal course to offer as preparation for parents who wish to have their children baptized.

5. *Engaged couples*. Many people start coming to church services because they want to get married. Why not encourage those who are planning to marry in your church (or who are recently married) to attend the Alpha course?

One church leader attended an Alpha conference and returned home full of enthusiasm. He spoke about Alpha in the service the following Sunday and none of the congregation showed the slightest interest. He went home very discouraged. But he prayed. Then he thought, *I have married five young couples this year, and none of them are Christians or come to church. I will invite them.* He did, and four out of the five said they would come. They had a great time. Several gave their lives to Christ, three are now PCC members and one is the church treasurer.

6. *Occasional churchgoers*. Many people go to church at Christmas, Easter, Harvest Festival or for family services. These are ideal opportunities to reach out to those who may not normally come to church. An appropriate talk may refer to the Alpha course, or we might

advertise via bulletin boards or other forms of publicity. At Christmas, for example, we give away copies of *Why Christmas?* (with an invitation to the next Alpha course) at the end of the service.

7. *The church magazine.* If you have a church or community magazine, use it to publicize your course. Printing interviews with those who have come to Christ on the local Alpha course has proved a very effective method of encouraging others to come along. This method may reach those who only have contact with the church through the church magazine. If you have not already run an Alpha course, it might be useful to use testimonies from other churches or stories from *Alpha News* or the book *The God Who Changes Lives.* (Please contact the publisher for permissions.)

8. *Community groups (Scouts, mother and toddler groups, marriage and parenting courses).* A number of churches are now involved in community activities. Drop-ins for the homeless, coffee mornings for mothers and toddlers and marriage and parenting courses are increasingly popular with nonchurchgoers. These provide the ideal setting to mention or even run the Alpha course.

9. *Guest services.* Guest services are aimed specifically at non-churchgoers and can be held on the Sunday before the Alpha course starts. We make sure that the date of the service is published in good time and encourage the regular members of our church to bring their friends. The service is broadly similar to a normal Sunday service and the key is to make it as nonthreatening and welcoming as possible. Many people come to Alpha as a result of attending a service like this.

Personal stories of changed lives are a key element of guest services. They are a powerful way of encouraging people to come to Alpha and are very easy to arrange. We try to find people who would be attractive to our guests—people with "street cred." If you haven't run Alpha before, perhaps ask someone from another church to come and give their testimony. We don't give them too much notice—testimonies are often most effective when they are spontaneous. We use an interview style, and keep the interview questions simple.

We use three very basic questions along these lines:

- Were you a Christian/churchgoer six months ago?
- How did you come to do Alpha? What happened on the course?
- And what difference has Jesus made in your life?

It is a good idea to promote the service with printed invitations or even an advertisement in the church magazine, bulletin, or local newspaper. We would also recommend having an "Alpha team" present at the end of the service to answer questions and hand out invitations to the next Alpha course with copies of *Why Jesus?*

10. *Alpha Sundays.* An Alpha Sunday is usually held the week before the guest service, and is a normal Sunday service with a ten-minute slot about Alpha. It aims to encourage members of your congregation to invite their friends to the guest service the following week and to your next Alpha course. This usually takes the form of a brief explanation of what the course entails and a couple of testimonies from the last course. We hand out an invitation to the forthcoming Alpha course with the service bulletins and publicize the guest service, which will take place the following week, to remind the congregation to bring their friends.

11. *Outreach and evangelistic events.* Alpha is an ideal follow-up course for an outreach event and has been used in this way by Luis Palau, J. John, and other evangelists. If you have a local mission event, church outreach or other community activity in your area, you could use the Alpha course as a follow-up to the event, encouraging all those at the event to explore the Christian faith further at an Alpha course in their local church. It is good to ensure that details of local Alpha courses are available at the event.

12. *Family life courses.* Increasingly, we are finding that these courses are providing a source of new people. Some people would not come to an Alpha course but they know they need help with their marriage or with parenting, for example. Nicky and Sila Lee run The Marriage Course at Holy Trinity Brompton in a similar way to the Alpha course in the sense that people come and have a meal, hear a talk, have coffee, and go into small groups. The only difference is that the small group has two members: a husband and a wife. They have various exercises that

they work through together. It has proved very successful with people outside the church. Increasingly, I think, people are recognizing that marriage is one of the really important things that we do that we get no training for in our society and we need help. It is not an admission of failure to go to a marriage course. Actually, it is a sensible thing to do—even if a marriage is very successful, it could be more successful, it could always be better.

We get people at all stages—people whose marriages are very good right through to people who are on the brink of divorce—coming on the course. Often at the end, they say, "We love this. We really enjoyed it." Maybe, during the course they heard a little bit about Alpha and they say, "Now we would like to do an Alpha course." We always have a number of people on Alpha who have come from The Marriage Course. Now it is also two-way traffic: there are people who come on Alpha who say, "We need help with our marriage." So they are going from The Marriage Course to Alpha and from Alpha to The Marriage Course.

13. *The Internet.* Increasingly, the most effective way of communicating is via the web and social networks, such as Facebook and Twitter. We have found these to be effective tools for engaging with a growing online community, as guests can easily extend information and invitations to courses and events.

Alpha.org is designed to be a guest-friendly site where guests can easily find Alpha courses in their local area by entering their zip code in the "find a course" section. There are tens of thousands of hits every month, and we are continuing to work on increasing traffic to the site.

We would highly recommend registering your Alpha course if you have not yet done so. This means that your details are recorded on alpha.org, helping potential guests in your area to find a course. We hear numerous testimonies of those who have come to Alpha via the information freely available on the Internet.

14. *Caring for Ex-Offenders (CFEO).* Over 15,000 people have done the Alpha course in prison in the U.K. Large numbers of them are now coming out of prison and are being reintegrated into the local Christian community through the CFEO ministry.

Over the years we have had a total thirty-eight ex-offenders in our own congregation, and it has been such a blessing to witness the transformation in their lives. Many of these have invited huge numbers of their friends onto the Alpha course and to our church. Several of them have helped on Alpha and a number of them have been regular members at our church for a long time. Linking an Alpha course to a CFEO program has been an effective way to see lives changed and many have subsequently attended an Alpha course as a result.

15. Using promotional resources
- Church sign—It is a widely held opinion in the advertising business that churches have the greatest under-used advertising resource: church sign on main roads up and down the country.
- Posters—Posters in the windows of church members' homes are a good source of free advertising and will let all the neighbors know about Alpha. If every person who had done Alpha in the U.K. (over 1.5 million people) was to put a poster up in their window, that in itself would have a major impact. Posters can also be placed in shop windows, libraries, pubs, coffee shops, offices, and factories—with permission!
- Car magnets—A relatively inexpensive way of advertising.
- Leaflets to homes—Recently a church in Ealing wanted to reach as many people as possible so they paid for a leaflet drop to 10,000 houses in their community at a cost of £200. As a result sixty-five unchurched people came to their Alpha dinner, fifty of whom went on to do the course itself. Most of them had no Christian background whatsoever.
- Social networking—Advertising on social networking sites such as Facebook has proved very effective, especially among the younger generation. A course in Brighton placed an advertisement on Facebook for anyone registered as living in Brighton and Hove aged between eighteen and forty. Within two weeks the advertisement popped up on Facebook profiles 5.5 million times. Anyone who clicked on the advertisement was directed straight through to alpha.org where they could connect to a local course. In two weeks, 651 people clicked through to alpha.org in response to the advertisement. To connect with Alpha on social networks, visit facebook.com/alpha and twitter.com/alpha.

- Participate in the Alpha Initiative—The Invitation is a combination of nationwide advertising with the personal invitation and has been instrumental in raising the profile of Alpha for thirteen years. Since the launch of Alpha Initiatives in 1998, we have witnessed a noticeable rise in the number of people attending Alpha in those countries where the Initiative is run. In the UK there has been a doubling of the number of nonchurchgoers attending the course—it is estimated that over 2.5 million people have now attended the Alpha course and 24 percent (18 million worldwide) of the U.K. adult population now recognize Alpha as a Christian course.

Most people attend an Alpha course as a result of a personal invitation. The role of advertising is to make the personal invitation easier. There are five benefits of advertising:

- It confers a sense of legitimacy. The average person concludes that something significant must be happening when they see extensive coverage of the course.
- Those who have done Alpha are encouraged to invite others because of the reinforcement of the media.
- It provides a conversation starter. Billboards, church notices or posters in people's homes make it easier to say, "Oh, have you seen that billboard or poster? That's what we're running in our home this week. Would you like to come?"
- If someone has received a leaflet, seen the billboards or posters, and read about Alpha in the newspaper, it may plant the idea that they would like to go. This makes them more likely to respond to the personal invitation.
- Advertising raises spiritual issues in the media and is likely to get people talking and make them more open to an invitation.

However, advertising does not work alone. It must be complemented by Christians actually inviting friends, family, and colleagues to Alpha.

Selecting a team

When starting an Alpha course, the first task is to choose a leadership team. If the course is going to be a large one (thirty plus) the team will need to include a director and possibly a worship leader.

Approximately one third of the course members should be the hosts and helpers. Each small group is made up of around twelve people of whom three or four are hosts and helpers. We have found that these people need to be selected very carefully. The hosts must be those who appear to have the beginnings of a gift of evangelism. They do not necessarily need to be Christians of many years' standing, but one indication of this gift is that they are "good with people." This is the test I often use when someone suggests someone, say Jane, as a host: "Suppose you had a nonchurchgoing friend for whom you had been praying for several years; would you be totally confident about putting them in Jane's group?" If the answer is "No," Jane is probably not suitable to be a host of a small group on Alpha. If the answer is "Yes," then Jane is likely to be a good host.

In every group we also have one or two helpers, usually one man and one woman. They might be a married couple or two single people. We do, however, try not to have a boyfriend and girlfriend hosting or helping with a group, as complications can arise if the relationship breaks up halfway through the course. The ideal is to have one couple and two single people on the leadership team of each group.

The helpers should pass the same test as the hosts, but they may be relatively new Christians. Indeed, occasionally they may not even be Christians at all. Many of our helpers are those who have just finished the previous course. Some ask to come back and do the course again. In many cases we would ask them to come back as helpers. We strongly discourage anyone from simply repeating the course. We do not want people to get stuck doing Alpha over and over again—they need to move on in their journey of faith, and one of the ways of moving on is to come back and help others. People who have recently done the course are often especially sensitive to the fears and doubts of members in their group. They can empathize with them, saying, "I felt that," or, "I found that difficult." This removes the "us" and "them" barrier.

As well as those who request to come back, we ask the hosts of the previous course to recommend those from their small group who they think would be good at helping. I myself look out for those I think would make good helpers and ask them to come back and help. Many of them are new Christians and many have lots of friends who are not Christians. A group of "happening" people attracts other people. Quite a high percentage of the next course will be friends of those who are helping. This is one of the ways in which the course grows. I have observed that those in the 18–35 age group generally have the largest groups of friends, and that many of them are still "open-minded" about their worldview. We have found that once people from this age group come to a course, numbers seem to rise more quickly. If we are to attract young people, we will need hosts and helpers in their age group.

I met someone named Nan Kirkland, who is eighty years of age. Nan has run Alpha nine times and has had over 250 people going through the course. She showed me a picture of her course, and my eyes popped out when I saw it, because in a group of thirty people, no one was over thirty apart from Nan. I didn't want to ask a rude question, but I said, "How did you get all these young people on the course?" She replied, "Well, I will not have any hosts or helpers over thirty on my course . . . most of my hosts are twenty or twenty-one and they attract the others."

Now, this doesn't mean to say that if we are over thirty there is nothing for us to do! Nan has proved that—she has herself a job! But she has seen that if we want to attract the young people outside the church, we need young hosts and young helpers.

Some people do not have the appropriate gifts or personality to be hosts and helpers. At times, we can make the mistake of thinking it would help them, even if they would not be the right person to help the guests. This is upside-down thinking —our focus should be our guests on Alpha. If people would not be suitable hosts or helpers, we have found it much more positive to suggest that their gifts be used in other areas of the course, for example on the "taskforce."

The taskforce is made up of a group of people who perform practical tasks such as catering, cleaning up, and moving chairs. They are vital to the smooth running of the course. They do not take part in the small groups, as they are fully occupied with the practical tasks. We have a dynamic group on the taskforce. They are people who either do not want to be in a small group or would not be suitable for a small group but have "the gift of helping others" (1 Corinthians 12:28). They are like the group chosen in Acts to "wait on tables" (Acts 6:2). They are men and women who are full of the Spirit and willing to serve in any capacity. Their love and service are in themselves a powerful witness to the love of Christ to those who are on the course.

A Catholic priest from one of the first Catholic parishes to run Alpha came to an Alpha conference at Holy Trinity Brompton. He went back and ran Alpha in his parish and it was a great success. I asked him whether he was giving the talks on the Alpha course, and he replied, "No, I do not give the talks. I do not feel that is particularly my gift." I went on, "Are you hosting a group on the course?" and he said, "No, I do not feel that is particularly me." So I said, "Are you involved?" and he said, "Oh yes, I am involved. I cook the food and I clear up afterwards. That is what I feel my gifts are. I love to be involved, I love everyone to know that I am supporting it, but that is my gift."

It showed extraordinary humility to be willing to do that. And I am not surprised to hear how well his course is working and how many people are coming to Christ through it. He loves Alpha because he sees people's faith in Christ coming alive and he enjoys using one of his gifts—I am sure he has many, many other gifts—and he loves watching other people using their gifts.

Training the team

Our latest research has shown that 26 percent of churches that are running Alpha do not run any team training. It breaks my heart to hear that! If the team is not trained, the small groups are very unlikely to work well. It is so sad to have gone to so much trouble to get the people there and then not to give them the best possible experience.

It is vital that all the team (especially those who have been Christians for many years) are trained each time we run an Alpha course. Hosts and helpers are invited to the training sessions. We run three evenings of training. Two are usually held on the two Wednesdays before the course begins. The first talk is on hosting small groups (see Chapter 7). The second is on pastoral care (see Chapter 9). The third training session is usually held on a Monday evening, just before the first weekend away. This session is on the subject of prayer ministry (see Chapter 13). These training evenings are opportunities for the teams to get to know one another before the Alpha course starts and for them to get together to pray for the course.

On the training evenings we meet at 7:00 P.M. for dinner. It is important that the team spend time together and get to know each other before the course begins. We don't assume that they already know each other very well. At 7:30 P.M. we begin with worship and prayer. All the way through we stress the importance of praying for the course. We then have a talk and an opportunity to ask questions either relating to the talk or about any other aspect of the course. At this point we cover some of the administrative details and prepare people for the jobs they will be asked to do on the first evening and thereafter. We aim to finish each training session at 9:30 P.M.

After Alpha

In practice, the strong friendships often formed on Alpha mean that the small groups want to stay together afterwards. However, new Christians need to be integrated into the life of the Christian community, and the appropriate ways of doing this will vary. With thousands of Alpha courses now running, there have been many requests for more follow-up material suitable for use in a pastorate or home group setting. In response to this, we have compiled a program of adult Christian education which now includes the following: Term 1 *The Alpha Course* (based on *Questions of Life*), Term 2 *A Life Worth Living*, Terms 3–4 *The Jesus Lifestyle*, Term 5 *Searching Issues*, Term 6 *God at Work* and Term 7 *The Heart of Revival*.

These resources aim to give people solid biblical roots for their new faith and lifestyle, and to address problems and difficult issues in a clear and simple way.

Conclusion

Sometimes people ask me whether Alpha is always a success story. They want to know if every person who comes on the course becomes a Christian, is filled with the Spirit, gets excited about Jesus, and brings hundreds of friends to the next course. Unfortunately the answer is, "No, it's not always like that!" Surveys from recent courses have shown that approximately 25 percent of the guests had dropped out. When we analyzed why, we found the following reasons.

First, they stopped coming because of us. We did not run the course as well as we might have done. For this reason we have questionnaires at the end of the course so that we can constantly improve it and make it more user-friendly (see Appendix E).

Second, people drop out for legitimate reasons. For example, some move to another part of the country. Increasingly, however, people are able to carry on with the course when they move. I know of one couple who started the course in London and finished it in Hong Kong! Another man did Weeks 1–7 at HTB, Week 8 in Boston, where he was on business, and then finished the course with us in London. This shows the advantage of the online Alpha Directory.

Third, people drop out for reasons connected with the parable of the sower (Matthew 13:3–8, 18–23). Jesus said that some people's hearts are hard: they are simply not ready to hear and they may leave after the first evening. Sometimes they come back on the next course, or a year later. One person came back after four years and said to me, "I have never forgotten what I heard the first night."

Some drop out because of personal troubles in their lives, or through persecution or ridicule. Somebody may laugh at them and say, "What are you doing going to church on a Wednesday?" Many of the people who come on the course lie about what they're doing on Wednesday nights. One man told me that a friend of his had come from New Zealand and asked him out for a drink on a Wednesday night. As he was going to Alpha he gave a vague excuse; he was not prepared to admit what he was doing. So his friend said, "Oh that's a pity," and he looked through his calendar, and asked, "How about next Wednesday?" He explained that he was busy, but had difficulty justifying why he was busy the next Wednesday and the next. Finally he admitted to being on a course. "What course is that?" the friend asked. "Oh," he replied, "I am learning French."

Jesus also outlines another category of people for whom the cares of this world, the delight in riches and the desire for other things come in and choke the Word. We have found that a new relationship or success at work or some other distraction may take people away either during or even after the end of the course.

And that leaves the last category, which Jesus called the good soil. A recent Alpha group that I was involved in was, in some ways, extremely discouraging! By the end of the course, only one person remained, apart from the hosts and helpers. His name was David. He was a futures broker and a commuter, and had sat opposite the same man on the train for many years. Being typically English, they had never spoken to each other, as they had not been introduced! However, they met at a party, they were introduced, and ultimately David went to work for Nick. They were having lunch together one day, and David asked Nick how he coped in such a highly pressured job. Nick replied, "Actually, it's God." The consequence of this conversation was that David came on the Alpha course.

One evening, about three or four weeks into the course, David had not said much. When someone asked him how he was, he explained that he had been for a physical in order to start his new job. The doctor had subsequently called him to say that one of his liver counts was over ten times too high: he would die in six months if he didn't stop drinking. Only David's close family knew that he was an alcoholic, and his marriage was under a lot of strain. The group hosts offered to pray for David, for him to receive Christ and for his addiction to be broken. David was, in his own words, "somewhat sceptical," but thought that anything was worth a try. The next day at work he was amazed to look at his watch and see that it was 2:00 P.M. Previously, he would have felt an overwhelming desire for a drink by then, but this day there was nothing. The following week David explained what had happened. He said that each time he felt the emptiness that usually caused him to reach for a drink, he read his Bible. His wife was furious that he had done this for God when she had been asking him for twenty years! She did, however, come to the celebration dinner, and brought their two children, aged twelve and fifteen. When I was chatting with her, she said that David was a different man; she now had a husband and the children had a father.

It was not difficult to persuade David's wife, Anne, to do the next course. The children got involved too, telling their school—friends what had happened to them. Next, David's sister did Alpha, having seen the change in her brother. Then a couple came to Alpha, simply because they had heard David's story. One helper brought her husband, who was also an alcoholic, and he too was set free from alcoholism. Another couple, who had dropped out of the Alpha course, came back to see what had happened to David, and went on to complete another Alpha course. By now, David and Anne's marriage had been totally transformed by the Holy Spirit. They then led an Alpha group together; not one person dropped out!

The seed that falls on good soil bears fruit thirty-fold, sixty-fold or, in David's case, a hundred-fold.

THE STORY OF
GRAM SEED

CHAPTER 6

GRAM SEED

For three years Gram Seed lived day and night on a bench outside a small shopping arcade in Middlesbrough. In 1996, he lay close to death and God intervened in an extraordinary way . . .

I was brought up by my grandparents and for many years I didn't know why. When I was nine, my grandad told me that my dad was quite violent and used to beat my mom up.

My nana was quite ill and suffered from depression a lot. In Middlesbrough we have a local psychiatric hospital called St. Luke's, and my nana was a day patient there all her life. She went to that hospital every day apart from the weekends, and sometimes she would go in for months. They would give her terrible electric treatments and I would hate to see the effect they would have on her. It really was barbaric and they don't do it now.

When I was eight, my mom got married to another fellow and moved out to a house about two miles away. It was never suggested that I would go and live with them, so I stayed with my nana and grandad, whom I loved. I felt that the new fellow never wanted me as part of the deal. As I grew up, I remember noticing that everyone else seemed to have moms and dads and brothers and sisters and stuff. It made me feel a bit like a freak, particularly as I knew other people thought of us as a bit like the Addams Family.

My nana was a bit of a drinker and used to keep 24-pack cans of lager under her bed. When I was about ten, I stole one of her cans and drank it. Then I went out for a walk and had a cigarette. As I was walking down the park, this bully from another neighborhood who was about three years older than me tried to get some cigarettes off me. I was really angry and I punched him. He hit the floor and then ran off. But the next day I noticed that everyone was talking to me and including me far more. I thought, *Why does everyone want to hang out with me now? It must be because I hit that kid.* So from then on I started fighting a lot. My uncle, Terry, was absolutely crazy about Bruce Lee and I used to watch the movies with him. I would practice the moves and became a really good boxer as well.

From about the age of twelve, I became a skinhead and started breaking into schools and stealing stuff. I started with my own school, stealing the saws, screwdrivers, and stuff. Then I moved on to other schools and youth clubs. We would go through the windows, opening them from the outside with a piece of wire. Then at the weekend we would sell anything we took.

I was treated as quite a madman because I wouldn't let anyone close to me. I grew up learning never to be afraid of anything, and would fight a lot with anyone on the street. My muscles were starting to come out and I was getting bigger and bigger. When I was about fourteen years old, I started hanging out with these guys from another neighborhood who took magic mushrooms, which they picked off the hill nearby. They make you hallucinate and do strange things.

When I was fifteen I was charged with twenty-two offenses of breaking into schools and youth clubs—but I had done many more than that. Me and the guys—three of us—would do it every night. We even stole cars, although we couldn't really drive. We wouldn't break into houses, though.

A few months later, while I was on bail, I was involved in a fight on a bus with another gang. There were about fifty of us in all – including punks and skinheads—when suddenly the bus started moving and we all thought it was time to get off in case the police came. As we leapt off, one guy from the other gang accidentally slipped under the wheels of the bus and was killed. That night the police came to arrest me and said, "We're charging you with murder." But I wasn't the only suspect and in the end no one was charged with that.

Nevertheless, I was classed as one of the hardest guys of my age in Middlesbrough. I was known as a bit of a psycho as I was not scared of anyone. I was sentenced to nine months in a detention center for the burglaries—and served seven months—but little changed after I was out. I just went back to the same old lifestyle. Soon after I came out of prison, my grandad died of a massive heart attack and the family just fell to bits. He had gone into hospital for an operation and I never even went to visit him. I was just too consumed with my own life. When he died, I was really tortured, because I felt I had let him down by being in trouble all my life. At the same time, a lot of the family blamed me for putting pressure on him.

After that, they sold our nana's house and I had nowhere to live. I stayed in loads of different places. By then, I had got introduced to fighting at soccer matches. I was never very interested in soccer because I thought it was for wimps, but then this kid said to me, "Yeah, but there's lots of fighting and that." So I thought, *I'll come to that*. And I thought it was great. Middlesbrough was in the old first division then and I would go every Saturday—or sometimes Tuesday nights. It was at soccer that I got slashed across the face with a knife, had a bottle stuck in my eye and chin, got four of my teeth knocked out, and got another big scar on my left arm from a police Alsatian dog.

I went to live in St. Hilda's—an area of Middlesbrough known as "over the border"—one of the roughest parts, with a family named the Wards. My nana moved in with my mom, but I didn't because I didn't really get along with my stepdad and I don't think they wanted me there. I knew my nana loved me, but she was very ill. She would give me money and that on a weekend. By then I wouldn't let anyone get close to me, no one—even though I would pick up loads of girls all the time. I got quite good at robbing—stealing stuff like T.V.s out of the back of trucks or all the cigarettes out of clubs.

A year later I had enough to buy my own house in Middlesbrough. I was right in the middle of organized crime in Middlesbrough. I was selling counterfeit perfume, counterfeit Lacoste tracksuits and T-shirts, counterfeit money, and all kinds of things. I was right in the middle of it all. I always seemed to have like loads of money—I had gold rings on every finger, a Rolex watch, Giorgio Armani suits—but I would squander it. I would smoke cannabis all the time and would often be out of my head on drugs.

When I was nineteen, I was staying at my mom's overnight when my nana died. It was a terrible shock, but it was made worse because my nana's wallet went missing at the time. Every single person thought I stole it and I must have scared her and that's why she died. It was all completely untrue, but when the police wanted to interview me, I just got completely drunk. In the middle of the night I caused a bit of a commotion by waking up everyone in my mom and stepdad's house. My stepdad was furious, so I hit him. After that, I started smashing the house up by hitting the walls and smashing my fists through the doors. I was taken away by the police. My mom and stepdad got an injunction on me, banning me not only from their house but the whole town where they lived.

Soon after that I got into a fight with the police at a soccer match and got two years in prison, where I served eleven months. I was totally drunk and high when it happened. They smashed up my house, pulling up the floorboards and everything, searching for evidence, and the house ended up being sold. I came out of prison just before my twenty-first birthday and made a bit of a truce with my mom again. She gave a great birthday party for me in Middlesbrough, but I had nowhere to live. I was big by now—six foot five with a 62-inch chest and 21-inch biceps. I had been training all my life and was muscly—I weighed twenty-one stone.

After that, I was basically sleeping anywhere I could for a night and needed money, so I was soon back involved in crime and stuff. That meant more time in jail, where I spent a lot of the next years. I was always fighting in jail, and often with prison officers—anyone who stood for authority. That meant time in solitary confinement, where I would get beaten up by the officers. That was how I got more of my teeth knocked out.

While in solitary, I used to "smoke the Bible"—using the paper to roll cigarettes, you got to smoke it. I used to shave my head bald, totally bald, because you weren't allowed to have your head shaved bald. You also had to have your shirt collar down, your top button fastened and your shirt tucked in, so I would put my collar up and pull my shirt out. They used to tell me to put it back in and I wouldn't—so I would go to my cell. Then the next time I'd be let out of my cell I'd "kick off," which meant I'd throw my dinner at them or kick the server over with all the food on it. Then they shut you in solitary. When you are let out, you go to the governor, and he'd say, "Right, I'm going to add thirty days on to your prison sentence."

I'd say, "So what?" and would walk away.

At that, he'd say, "I'm not going to be abused."

I'd say, "Well you are, because I'm going to make your life hell." And I did make their lives hell while I was in there. I just hated them.

In 1990, I got out of jail again and got a job as a doorman in a nightclub. It was hard work, but it kept me out of trouble . . . until New Year's Day 1991. A fight broke out on the dance floor of the club and I moved in. What I didn't know was that two undercover coppers were circulating the pubs and clubs that night—and I hit one of them hard and he went down. I had no idea he was a cop. It could only happen to me. I just put my hands up and said, "Look, I didn't know they were cops. I thought it was the best thing to do, you know." I got twelve months for that. I did six months out of the twelve and when I came out I decided to end it all. I sat down on a bench near an arcade of shops in Middlesbrough one night, and I took out my knife with a twelve-inch blade and cut my wrists. I woke up in hospital with a cop sitting next to me. The police had actually thought someone was trying to murder me—but I didn't know that. So when I saw the cop, I pulled the drip out and took off.

I was later found and put into the psychiatric hospital, St. Luke's— the same place my nana had been in. By now I was hearing voices and stuff and drinking cider and generally becoming more and more of a bum. When I came out of St. Luke's in 1993, the council gave me a place near the bench where I had cut my wrists—but I didn't want to live in it. By now I was just sick of life—totally sick of it. I didn't want to leave St. Luke's because I'd already been acclimated to it—not having any pressure. So at the end of 1993, I decided to stay on my bench and just drink myself to death. I also injected heroin, sniffed cocaine, sniffed paracetamol, drank meths . . . I just sat on this bench drinking and drinking and drinking. For a long while I just wore a T-shirt—in the cold and rain and snow and frost with just a T-shirt. Then one of the guys in the town (named Dale) came up to me one Christmas and said, "What's happened to you, my friend?" and all that. Then he gave me $35 and put a $400 jacket around me—which I went and sold for another $35.

I stayed on that bench day and night until 1996—apart from the odd night when I would go to my flat to warm up. But the prostitutes would use my flat for their business, so there were always people there. Kids used to spit at me and throw things at me and slap my head around and flick cigarettes at me. I'd become a tramp. I used to poo myself and wee myself. I was just a stench. I talked to myself the whole time. I would beg and people would give me pound coins and other cash, but otherwise no one would bother with me. I was a chronic alcoholic and I was ready to die. I used to drink twenty-eight to thirty pints of White Lightning every day, which I could afford because of my begging. I even stole from the collection plate at the back of one of the churches to pay for my drinking.

It was one night in March 1996 that a group of around eight people came along and they were talking to the prostitutes and that. I was on my bench and two of the guys came over to me. One said, "I just want to tell you Jesus loves you."

I said, "What?" and started swearing at him and telling him to go away. And they went away.

The next Friday they came back and said, "Look, Jesus loves you, really, you know." I told them to get away again and said I didn't want to know about Jesus. They seemed to have this type of boldness about them as though they weren't really scared. But I think they were wary of me. After that, I started seeing these guys everywhere I went. Everywhere. I'd never seen them before. I would walk from my bench through the town and suddenly one of them would say, "Hey Gram, how are you doing?" Sometimes they would give me a lift in a car if I wanted to go and see one of my friends in a pub. I would often go and see them on payday, because I knew they'd look after me.

One night I burned my leg quite badly on the electric fire in my flat because I fell asleep against the bar. These Christians, Peter and Aiden, came up to me on the bench later and said, "Gram, have you seen your leg?" They took me to hospital, but when the nurse looked at me she said, "The worst thing we're going to have to do is to surgically remove your socks." I had worn the socks for five or six months without changing them, and my skin had grown over my socks. In the end, they could only take them off with a scalpel. I went back to the bench but some time later, in late 1996, I collapsed in the flat and no one could wake me. They called the ambulance and when I got to the hospital, they found I had septicaemia, pneumonia, hypothermia, severe malnutrition, severe dehydration and my liver and kidneys had failed (apart from that I was okay!).

I was in a coma and on the fifth night of the coma they got my mother into a room with my stepdad and said, "As his only legal guardian, we are advising you to allow us to switch the ventilation machine off that's keeping him breathing, because there's nothing we can do for him now."

She thought about it and said, "Look, I want you to keep trying—at least till you've got some more proof."

Two hours later they took my mom back into this room and said, "We've tried some more tests on your son and he's still not responding. We've tried to get him to respond to treatment for five days, and he isn't. There's no oxygen in his blood, and the short of it is that even if he wakes up, he's going to be paralyzed from the neck down. It is only the machine that is keeping him breathing."

And my mom said, "I don't care. You fight for him. There's breath there—keep fighting."

The following day, the Christian guys, Pete and Aiden and the others, arrived at the hospital. They had missed me on my bench and had been asking around about what had happened to me. So they came to the hospital and asked my mother what happened. She told them and they said, "Can we pray for him?"

Mom said, "Yeah, of course. I don't know what you mean by 'pray for him,' but go for it."

So they put their hands on me and said, "In the name of Jesus Christ of Nazareth, give this man new life."

And I woke up. My eyes opened at once and I started breathing by myself. I slipped back to sleep, but I stayed breathing on my own after that. It was after another two days that I woke up and I said to my mom, "What happened?"

She said, "These guys prayed for you."

I said, "Who did they pray to?"

"God."

"God?!"

"Yes, Jesus."

And I said, "What does Jesus want to know about a scumbag like me for? I thought he only liked nice people who went to church and didn't swear and spit and fight."

She said, "I don't know son, you'd better ask them. They'll be back later. They've been in every day since they found out you were in here."

So when the guys came in, I asked them and they told me about Jesus coming and dying on a cross so that I could be forgiven. I remember pulling the sheets up and laughing. They kept coming as long as I was in hospital and they never pushed it about Christianity. They used to just come and sit with me and chat with me. And I used to think it was great. When I got out of hospital, I couldn't walk properly. I had two walking sticks and had to go downstairs on my seat. I was really weak. I got a room with one of my old friends—but I still saw quite a bit of the Christian guys, who would come and visit. I would often ask them questions about this Jesus.

Then one day one of them said, "Look, you're asking loads of questions. Why don't you come on an Alpha course at our church?" He explained it was a course where you could ask all these kinds of questions. I thought, *Church? You're joking, aren't you?* But in the end I agreed to give it a try. So I went to Alpha and there were about sixty people in this room—young and old—and I thought, *What a load of rubbish—but at least the food's good.* At the group, they seemed to be just talking a lot of garbage about this Jesus fellow and I was swearing— just laughing at them.

The following Wednesday I went back and it seemed a bit easier. I was still swearing and felt like I had nothing to say. At one point, I left the room and wandered down this corridor looking for the safe, because I thought I would take the money. I came to a locked door and thought, *Shall I get my knife out and open the door?* Then I thought, *Nah, I'll leave it* and I went back to the group. By now, I was really cleaned up and friends had given me nice clothes and even paid for a haircut. I felt really great and even started looking forward to Wednesdays, because it was a night out and I felt good. I remember saying to a friend named Lizzie, "I think I should see a psychiatrist."

She said, "Why?"

I said, "Well, you know this Christian place? I've just had a bath and a shave and I can't wait to get there."

She said, "Ah, it'll go. It'll pass. Don't worry. It's just a new thing. You'll get there tonight and then the next week it'll wear off. Don't worry about it." By now, I didn't want to swear when I was at Alpha because I could see these were nice people—but I couldn't stop, however hard I tried.

One night after Alpha, one of the Christian guys, Martin, said, "Why don't you come back to my house tonight and meet my wife and have coffee and some cake?" So I went back and was there till 12:30 that night—just talking. Martin wasn't bothered about me swearing and his wife wasn't bothered about me swearing. I couldn't stop.

Then came the Alpha Day Away. I was in two minds whether to go or not, but I thought, "It's a day out anyway—and all the group's going and there'll be loads of food." We listened to these talks about the Holy Spirit and that afternoon —it was a quarter to three on November 9, 1996—Martin, who was leading, said, "If you want to receive a gift, it's normal to put your hands out . . ." He explained that it was sometimes the same with receiving the Holy Spirit. Then he invited the Spirit to come.

I put my hands out and I remember saying to Jesus, "Jesus, if this is real, if it's true what these guys have said—that you love me—then prove it. I want you to prove it to me."

And I just felt this indescribable love surging into my heart. I just got this love. It was all over me. I sat down and I was crying. I was really weeping—and I'd never cried for anyone, not even when my nana and grandad died. It was a weakness, crying. I mean, I cried when I was drunk—many times—when a leaf fell off a tree or a cat crossed the road. But if you're drunk then you cry about everything. But this time I was sober and I was weeping. I was just saying to God, "Thank you. Thank you." I just felt so wanted, so needed. Then Martin led me in a prayer, when I said, "Dear Jesus, I acknowledge that You died for me. Please forgive me for not acknowledging You all my life and just ignoring You. Please come into my life and keep me free for ever. Amen."

I felt I belonged to someone at last. All my life I'd never belonged to anyone. I was a misfit and here I was belonging to someone. That night, I got home and said to my Christian friend, "Peter, you must take me to the center of Middlesbrough, I have to tell the prostitutes and the heroin addicts about Jesus, because He's real." And that Saturday night, I went out and told them all. I think they thought I was brain damaged. And do you know what else happened that day? I stopped swearing. It went—disappeared. To this day I've never sworn again. I don't even think about swearing. Jesus just took it away. Lying in bed that night, I prayed, "Jesus, I know You are real and that You died for me. From now on, every single day of my life, I'm going to go and tell everyone about You." I felt totally clean, totally washed. The following day, I went to church. I was very weak still, but I was getting better and better. Even my insides were all starting to work again.

My whole life started changing at once. Although I drank a vast amount and smoked like a chimney up until that day, I have never drunk or smoked a cigarette since. I finished the Alpha course and became a helper on the next one. And the more I did it, and the more I spent time with Christians, I just had this strong urge to love Jesus more, and to tell people more. Jesus was now my friend. I started praying regularly and although I couldn't read properly—and still can't—I still wanted to read the Bible and now have a large-print Bible. There is a Scripture that says, "Those who are forgiven much will love much" and it is true. I love everybody now. I never loved my mom or my stepdad, but I love them now. Because of the forgiveness that Jesus has given me, He has put a new love for people in my heart.

For years I sat on that bench thinking, "I want to die, I want to die." But now all I want to do is live because of what Jesus has done for me. It's just totally the opposite.

In 1999, Gram Seed married Natasha, whom he had met on a Christian training course. They now have two sons, Caleb and Boaz. Gram visits prisons on a regular basis to help with Alpha courses and to tell prisoners about Jesus Christ. Gram is the author of two books. Information about Gram's charity, Sowing Seeds Ministries, can be found at www.sowingseeds.org.uk

CHAPTER 7

HOSTING SMALL GROUPS

John, a TV executive in his thirties, came with his wife, Tania, to an Alpha dinner at the end of a course. Tania decided she wanted to do the next course, but John agreed to come along only reluctantly. He played little part in the discussion groups, apart from the occasional, rather negative, remark. On the weekend away he walked out of one of the sessions and told his wife they were leaving. She had become a Christian during the weekend and so was very disappointed to have to leave. Nevertheless, she agreed to go with him. He told her on the way home that he was going to give up going to Alpha. I had not been involved in the weekend but Tania told me on Sunday of John's decision. So on the following Wednesday I was amazed to see him walk through the door. Later in the evening, when we were in small groups, we went around the group, each person reporting on their experience of the weekend. When it came to John, he told us what had happened. Naturally, I asked him why he had come back. He replied simply, looking at the group, "I missed you lot."

In John's case it was the small group that kept him coming to Alpha. He later gave his life to Jesus Christ and he and his wife are now firmly involved in the church. This incident shows us the vital importance of the small group.

The overall purpose of the small group, along with the course as a whole, is to help to bring people into a relationship with Jesus Christ. Jesus Himself said that where two or three are gathered in His name He is there also (Matthew 18:20). We have found that a group of about twelve (comprising two hosts, two helpers and approximately eight guests) is the ideal size. I do not think it is a coincidence that Jesus chose a group of twelve (Mark 3:13–19).

The six aims of the small group

1. Discussion

The groups meet to discuss the talk and issues arising out of the talk. It is vital to give people the opportunity to respond to what they have heard and to ask questions. This is especially the case if the group is made up predominantly of those who are not yet Christians. Usually such groups are not ready to study the Bible. When we first ran Alpha courses, the groups always studied the Bible from the first week. I soon realized that this was leading to considerable frustration. When the questionnaires came back at the end of the course there were comments such as, "I only really enjoyed our group when we were allowed to spend the whole time discussing the talk." Another wrote, "I would have liked more time discussing the talk and more freedom to diverge from the set Bible study."

The practical details are very important. The chairs need to be arranged so that everyone is comfortable and can see one another. Light and ventilation need to be good. Everyone should have access to a modern translation of the Bible. A good host aims to keep the discussion to the set time. We aim to start at 9:00 P.M. and finish at 9:30 P.M. I discourage hosts from going on as a whole group beyond this time, even if they are involved in a rip-roaring discussion. It is always possible to say, "Let's continue this next week," which will encourage people to return to continue the debate. If the groups go on too long, people may be put off from coming back, fearing another late night.

Some groups are ruined by one of two things. First, ineffective leadership, where the host is not properly prepared or allows one person in the group to do all the talking. Or second, by an over-dominant host who does all the talking instead of giving those on the course the freedom to speak and to say what is on their minds. The host needs to be flexible enough to allow the group to change the subject, but confident enough to gently cut short "red herrings" that are frustrating the majority.

It is important to ask simple questions. If you feel that the group is not ready for Bible study but discussion is not flowing very easily, possible questions to start discussion are listed in Appendix I of the training manual. Two basic questions to ask are "What do you think?" and "What do you feel?"

Hosts need to be prepared to help bring out answers to the issues raised in the group. I have found that some questions come up time and time again. The book *Searching Issues*[1] looks at the seven issues most often raised on Alpha. I encourage the hosts and helpers to be familiar with this material as well as reading around each of the subjects in it.

A good host will always be an encourager. At the most basic level this means smiling at people and being and looking interested in what each person has to say. Even if someone says something that is not correct, a good host will respond with a phrase like "How interesting," or "I have never heard that before," or "It might mean that . . .," and will then bring in the rest of the group to try to reach the right conclusion.

2. To model Bible study

The second aim of the small group is to learn to study the Bible together and to grow in knowledge. As mentioned already, the host should encourage the group members to do most of the talking and must resist the temptation to give a sermon.

Even if a Bible study is planned, it is important to give an opportunity to ask questions arising from the talk and to deal with these first. Otherwise, members of the group may feel frustrated that the real questions on their hearts and minds are not being answered.

If the group is ready for Bible study, the host needs to prepare the passage carefully. He or she should read the passage in different versions and make sure they understand it. They should try and spot any difficult verses and look up the explanation in a commentary (in order to avoid wasting time in the group).

In the group setting, explain where the passage comes in the Bible and give the page number if using the same version, so that no one is embarrassed by their lack of knowledge. Sometimes it may be appropriate for each person to read a verse (for example, if you are looking at one of the Psalms); this gets everyone involved. For some passages (e.g., the prodigal son) it is better for the whole passage to be read by one good reader. Reading aloud can be a harrowing experience for some and they must be able to decline easily.

Then it is helpful to give a short introduction. For example, when studying the story of the prodigal son, one might begin by saying, "Obviously, the father represents God and the son represents us. Let us see what lessons we can draw from the passage." The introduction must be very short, perhaps one sentence, giving the main theme of the passage. It is a good moment to explain any obvious difficulties or ambiguous words. Hosts should be particularly careful to avoid using Christian jargon which excludes the nonChristian and the new Christian.

Next, the host has to get everyone talking. It is a good idea to work out the questions carefully in advance, and they should be kept short and simple. Questions that are either too vague (e.g., "What is the difference between verses 7 and 17?"), too easy (e.g., "Who died for us?"), or too difficult will not help to start discussion. Good questions to ask are open-ended ones that cannot be answered "Yes" or "No" and which provoke discussion of the key verses of the passage. The three basic questions to ask about any passage are "What does it say?", "What does it mean?", and "How does it apply to our lives?"

The aim is to bring everyone into the discussion. Contributions from the quieter members of the group should be especially welcomed. If one person has done a lot of talking, it is good to ask, "What do other people think?" Hosts should aim to learn as well as teach, and should not force their own ideas on the group. Even if we are asked directly for our own view, it is better, if possible, at first to deflect the question. Nor should we answer our own questions: it is better to re-phrase them.

Hosts should try not to repeat other people's comments unless they need clarifying for the rest of the group. If we are asked questions that we cannot answer it is fatal to bluff. We need to admit we do not know all the answers. Such an admission is often a good thing, and we can always tackle the question afterwards, or say that we will make a note of it and bring the answer next week. Better still, someone in the group might like to look up the answer. This helps the learning process, both for guests and for hosts. It is important we do not give the impression that there are easy answers to complicated questions or that we are great experts.

The most important thing is to make the study practical, so that everyone can see how they should apply the principles, and how God can use the passage to change their lives. There is no need to study for too long—thirty minutes is plenty.

3. To learn to pray together

If the host wishes to open in prayer, it must be done sensitively. The host may pray or, better still, ask a member of the group to do so. However, it needs to be done very carefully. They need to be asked beforehand and it needs to be made clear to the rest of the group that this is the case. Otherwise, people will be afraid that next time they themselves may be asked to open in prayer. (I know of one or two people who stopped coming because they thought they might have to pray aloud.)

To avoid embarrassment, the host could suggest a simple prayer (i.e., "Will you ask God to give us wisdom to understand this passage?"), or, having asked someone beforehand, say to the group, "I have asked X to open in prayer."

Later on in the course, it may be appropriate to end with prayer. As most people find praying out loud quite daunting in the initial stages, it is important to talk about these difficulties and then model a very simple prayer, like "Father . . . (short sentence) . . . for Jesus' sake. Amen." This will encourage others that they could do something similar. Long eloquent prayers may be impressive, but they discourage others from praying. If we provide a simple model I have found that virtually everyone in the group prays, sometimes even those who are not yet Christians.

For those who do take the step and pray their first, faltering prayer, it can be a momentous occasion, giving new confidence to their relationship with God. It is deeply moving to hear someone's first public prayer. It is usually completely uncluttered by jargon and obviously comes straight from the heart. It is good to make clear to people that we all benefit when they muster the courage to pray aloud, however briefly and simply.

4. To develop lasting relationships within the body of Christ

It has often been said, "People come to church for many reasons, but they stay there for only one: that they make friends." We have found that extraordinarily close friendships are made during the course of the ten weeks. Four years ago I had a small group of twelve people, none of whom were Christians at the start of the course, but by the end they had all come to faith in Christ. All are now in positions of Christian leadership and remain very close. Immediately after the course, one of them said that before it had begun he had felt his "friends register" was full and was amazed to find that he had made so many lasting relationships.

The hosts and helpers need to get to know each person in the group well. It is important to learn their names on the first night. Sometimes we play a name game to make this easier. Each evening the group sits together for dinner and the hosts and helpers act as hosts and facilitate the conversations. Sometimes the group will go for a drink at the end of the evening, if people are comfortable with that. Sometimes they will meet up during the week, either on a one-to-one basis or all going out together as a group.

5. To learn to minister to one another
One small group I was involved in recently started out full of questions, some of which were quite hostile. They all seemed so different that I began to wonder whether they would all get along together, let alone minister to one another in the power of the Holy Spirit. But by the end it was wonderful to see them all praying for each other, laying on hands and praying for healing.

6. To train others to host
Alpha has grown at such a rate that we continually need more hosts. It has grown from one small group to thirty-five small groups on the current course. Initially, the hosts were experienced Christians, often of at least ten years' standing. Many of the helpers these days have become Christians on the previous Alpha course and even the hosts may have been Christians for as little as six months. This is not ideal, but it is a good problem to have: presumably the early church was faced with a similar situation. When 3,000 were converted on the day of Pentecost some of them must have needed to lead virtually right away.

Paul tells Timothy to entrust the things he taught him "to reliable people who will also be qualified to teach others" (2 Timothy 2:2). It has been said that "Delegation without training leads to disappointment," and we make sure that all hosts and helpers have done the three-session Alpha Team Training course. The helpers can learn more about leadership from watching the hosts of their group "in action," and it is hoped that the hosts' model may one day be useful to all the group members.

THE STORY OF
DONNA MATTHEWS

CHAPTER 8

DONNA MATTHEWS

As a guitarist and vocalist with the band Elastica, Donna Matthews hit the big time when the group's debut album went straight to number one in the UK charts. But life was not easy. Here she tells the story.

My mom and dad divorced when I was about two and some four years after that my dad went to prison for drugs. I've got two sisters; Ceri is three years older than me and Lisa is a year younger. We grew up on a council estate in Bettws, South Wales, and then moved nearby to a village called Bishton.

Family life was good—we were really close. It was my mom and us three girls. We didn't have much money but we were quite a loving family and we'd often go and visit my dad on weekends. He was quite a long way away in prison in Dartmoor. He got moved a few times. He was in for about seven years. My dad played guitar and was interested in music and I think that's where I got my interest in music from.

My mom used to smoke dope and at about twelve I started smoking dope too. I became really rebellious—I got into drugs and music and the whole punk culture really. Around that time my dad came out of prison and got a house in Newport so I started going into town a lot more.

Me and my sister Lisa started busking in town and through that met older boys who had bands. We'd start hanging out with them and we lost interest in school. They also had access to harder drugs and by the age of fourteen I was doing acid and speed. Sometimes I'd sit in on my own on weeknights and take mushrooms or speed and then go to school the next day and sniff glue and aerosols. At that time I was self-harming as well and I got caught in school for cutting my arm. I was always in trouble for everything—for truancy, for writing on the desks, for shouting at teachers, for not paying attention and for stealing stuff from the classrooms.

My mom would say, "I can't control you. You're out of control." Sometimes she'd sit me down and say, "Look—this has got to stop. I can't take it."

I'd think, *I'll try, I'll try, I'll try* ... But then I couldn't.

When I was fourteen the school said that I'd have to leave if I didn't behave. I said, "Well, I'm gonna leave anyway." And I just left.

My mom then said, "Look, I can't take any more. You're uncontrollable. I want you to move to your dad's."

I was like, "Great." I had a lot more freedom living with my dad, I could do whatever I wanted really.

My dad was a rebel and he took drugs. He used to take me to nightclubs and things like that. When the truancy officers called at my dad's, he would say, "Oh, she's not staying here." When the authorities eventually caught up with me they put me into a special needs unit for wayward children in Hartridge, South Wales. I was fifteen by then. I had a boyfriend at the time and in the evenings I would go into Newport to see him.

At sixteen I was allowed to leave Hartridge and I moved into town. I didn't have any qualifications and I just started selling drugs. I started off by buying a bit of dope and selling that and then over the next couple of years I built up a business selling dope and speed. I ended up selling kilos of dope—like nine ounce bars—and I'd buy like two ounces of speed and I'd sell it in grams.

I did have some proper work—menial jobs like bar work and things like that—but basically I didn't know what I wanted to do. I was a bit lost. I knew I wanted to do music but I sort of lost all my confidence. I had been taking a lot of acid for a couple of years and had a bit of a breakdown. I got really disillusioned with life and started thinking, *What's the point of it all?* I had been writing songs since I was about ten and was still doing some music.

When I was seventeen, I bought an electric guitar and started playing that. I'd sit playing for hours and that became my solace really. I was living with a boyfriend in Newport, just above a nightclub.

Around that time I had a driving instructor who was a bit of a psychiatrist and he'd sort of counsel me a little bit. I'd say, "Society—

there's no point in it all. It's all useless. I'm into green politics."
He'd say, "Well, why don't you work for CND or Greenpeace?"
I'd say, "Yeah, but it's not worth it."
He'd say to me, "Look if you want to do something about a problem, you have to take action."

Bit by bit it started sinking in and so when I was about eighteen or nineteen I decided to go back to college. I thought, "I'm gonna go back and get a GED and then do a degree."

I started college—a tech in Newport—and made new friends. I then joined the college band and that was the beginning of a new era for me. I was still dealing dope but to a different crowd of people—less the sort of real manic drug heads to more like casual dope-smokers.

I then started playing in another band that I'd formed. It was good and I started thinking, "This is what I want to do." The first band had been sort of a covers band, but the second band was indie music like The Jesus and Mary Chain, Pixies, and Nirvana, which were all around then. That band was quite successful and it started making me think. For the first time I had hope. I could see a future and I started laying the foundations for what I wanted to do. I started taking art classes but I only got halfway through that and music sort of took over.

There had been a few arguments in our band and I thought, "I'm gonna go up to London and get a band together." It was around 1990. I was twenty years old. I'd been to London when I was younger but I didn't really have a clue. I knew of someone from Newport who'd moved to London and was in a band, so I got his number and asked if I could crash on his floor until I found somewhere to live—and that's what I did.

I then started looking through the back of music papers like the *NME* and *Melody Maker* and answered some ads and started auditioning. I auditioned for a band who was looking for a guitarist. The audition was at a place called The Premises down in Hackney. After half an hour they said, "Yep—cool" and that was it. There were three there; the bass player, Annie; the singer, Justine; and the drummer Justin. We later became Elastica. Our first gig was about eight months later. Me and Justine wrote all the songs. A lot of Justine's were about frustration and mine were about questioning my reality a bit. I think I was always looking at deeper meanings and things.

I was still doing drugs at this stage, but not heavily—I couldn't afford it. I'd smoke a bit of dope and maybe do some speed on the weekend but not heavy use. It was the same for the others. We started becoming successful and getting a bit more money. We were invited to more parties and the pressures grew. We would have to go from one thing to another and we were on the road a lot. We would be drinking one night and then the next day we'd be travelling again so we'd all be drinking and then you'd take drugs to counteract the alcohol. We would end up going on benders for a couple of weeks and have a week off. Bit by bit those stretches got closer and closer together.

After a couple of years in a band—and we'd started making a lot of money quite fast—we were on a continual bender. We would get through hundreds of pounds worth of drugs in a week. I was taking heroin by then. The other band members were doing it too. We all smoked it but I ended up getting into needles when I was about twenty-four or twenty-five.

Life in the band was what would be classed as glamorous. We had lots of money; we'd get planes here, there, and everywhere. We'd fly to this country and that just for a party. It was like a lot of drugs and excess really and it was supposedly fun but bit by bit I started feeling really, really empty. I had this double life. One day I'd be out doing a TV program or something and the next I'd be home down the Cross [Kings Cross] hanging round with crack addicts and going back to their squats. I'd bought the flat there because it was somewhere I could get drugs twenty-four hours a day. The more I got into that way of living, the more I retreated from any friends and the more drugs became my friends.

In the band we became more and more unfriendly because of the stresses. We started getting into a lot of arguments and would lie to each other all the time. At this stage we were supposed to be in a studio every day recording our second album. It was like a grand a day for the studio and we'd hardly turn up. The first album we produced—which was just called *Elastica*—went on and sold like a million copies. The second album took five years to make and then it dribbled out. I left the band in 1998 before it was released.

My heroin habit then started to become really debilitating. I got to the point where I didn't really leave my bedroom. I didn't really go out; I didn't answer the phone (I was scared of the phone)—I was paranoid, I was totally fearful and incapable of living. All I could do was get up and "use" and then I'd sleep, "use", sleep, "use." As well as heroin I'd be injecting speed. I'd take speed to help me get out and face the world and then gear to make me relax. I had lots of random boyfriends—no one meaningful.

Around that time I had a few breakdowns where I just couldn't cope. The fear just felt so extreme. One night when I'd taken heroin I even had an experience where I thought I'd gone to hell. It was a place with burning people—it was just horrible. When I came back to my room I was so scared I went straight out of my house without any shoes or socks on. I got in my car and drove to someone else's house. I was terrified. My mind started to go. I had tried for years to get clean. I kept saying, "I'm not going to use, I'm not going to use." And I'd try different things to get clean but every time I'd use again. I wanted to get clean because I knew it was killing me and I didn't like the person I was becoming. It was stealing my soul.

When I first took heroin it used to make me feel like I was in heaven. Then, as time went on, I'd feel fearful when I was taking it and even more fearful when I wasn't. Towards the end I would be absolutely beside myself with terror at facing the world when the heroin wore off. I'd feel so raw that I'd do almost anything for some heroin. I'd then take some more just to make the fear go away. It would be a relief to feel sort of normal again. I'd feel like a functioning person. I wouldn't feel high—it would just make me be able to sit in my skin.

People don't keep using because they want to but because they have to. Without it, it's like having a massive mental and physical breakdown. The pain of getting clean was harder than the pain of being on it. It seemed invincible.

At twenty-seven I decided to go back home to my mom in Wales and I was there for nearly six months—but I still couldn't get clean. I lied to my mom that I was clean and then she would find me using again. I just couldn't get back on my feet. She'd come into my bedroom and there'd be foil around me—and I'd be passed out. Soon after that I managed to get onto a treatment program to get off the heroin. It was for eight weeks at Barley Wood in Bristol. I thought, *This is my last chance.*

The treatment center was horrible—about four very sick people
to a room. It was a twelve-step treatment center, so it was based on
having a spiritual awakening to recover. Each day would start with
some sort of spiritual reading from a twelve-step book. After that
we'd have breakfast and then you'd have to do some Therapy Duties
(TDs): cleaning, washing-up, that sort of thing. We'd also have to make
our bed and tidy our room. Then we'd have an hour and a half of
teaching—normally something about addiction. I felt absolute terror
throughout this time. I was scared of everything and I was so ill. All
the people who had recovered said that they had prayed to God and
He had helped them to get clean—so I thought, *Right, I'm going to try
praying.*

One night I lay in bed and prayed. I just said, "If there is a God
and You can hear me, then please help me." I remember being quite
embarrassed when I prayed it. I then woke up in the middle of the
night and thought I wanted to go to the toilet. I sat in the toilet but
didn't want to go. As I sat there, I thought, *What am I doing?* I started
crying—and I cried and cried for ages. I then went back to bed and
when I got up in the morning I felt like something had changed in me.
That started me thinking, *Well if this God is real then I'd better find out
what God is.* I kept praying, "God show me."

From then on I went on a mission to know God and I started getting
better. When I finished the program I went to visit my family but when
I got there I just couldn't handle the emotions and I thought, *I need some
heroin, and I need it now.*

I stole my sister's car and went to the dealer's house in Newport. The
whole way in the car I was praying, "God please help me, please help
me, please help. Help me not to use."

I got to the dealer's house. The lights were on and I knocked on the
door. I could see the TV on but he didn't answer the door. I shouted
through the mailslot and he still didn't answer so I had to leave and I
drove back to my mom's house. I feel that God helped me that night.

After living in Bristol for about a month I returned to my apartment
in Kings Cross and started attending twelve-step meetings about twice
a day every day. I started doing music again and wrote a few songs. I
saw my old band and actually went to see them play. I got up on stage
with them. I think they were really pleased that I'd got clean. On the

twelve-step program you have to have a sponsor—someone who helps
you through the steps. My sponsor was a Christian. She took me to
church once but it didn't really mean that much. I wasn't interested.
I believed that God was a higher form of consciousness—part of me,
within me and in everything and everyone.

It wasn't a person, it was an energy or something like that. I basically
thought there were two energy forces in the universe —good and evil—
and God was the good force. Later, I started attending a food addiction
twelve-step program. I became a sponsor and my sponsee turned out
to be a Christian who attended a church called Holy Trinity Brompton.

In 2002, someone else from the twelve-step program mentioned to me
about the Alpha course at HTB and I thought, *I'll go.* I was quite cynical
and didn't think I needed Christianity in my life. But I had two friends
who were Christians and I thought they were lovely people—so I went.
I missed the first night of the course and started on the second week. I
went in and sat on the top balcony, which was full of people. There must
have been a couple hundred people there I think. I wasn't expecting
that. I thought there'd be a few somber-faced people, but instead it was
cool. I was introduced to my group, which included a couple of people
I recognized from the food twelve-step program I was in. I thought,
Hmmm. Fancy seeing you here . . . It was nice.

After the supper Nicky Gumbel got up to speak. He seemed to really
believe in what he was talking about and that inspired me. At the end
of his talk he gave people a chance to say a prayer to invite Jesus into
their lives. He said, "If anyone wants to offer their lives to Christ, to
get to know Christ, then just say 'I'm sorry for the things I've done' "
and he led people in the prayer. I said that prayer then but despite that,
I still questioned everything. I thought, *Maybe he's deluded. I think that
there's lots of paths to God and that's his truth.* It didn't make me want to
change my path.

In the group discussion we'd talk about things and I didn't really
feel like my questions were answered, but I'd voice them anyway.
Halfway through the course we went on the Alpha weekend about the
Holy Spirit. I was fine with it. Sometimes, if I was looking at a sunset
I'd pray and would feel a feeling of peace. That was my experience of
God's presence so I assumed the Holy Spirit thing would be something
like that.

The weekend was held in Pakefield, Suffolk. It was good, I liked it but I was still cynical. On the Saturday evening I was still quite cynical of everything. I thought, *I've experienced more Spirit than you.* I was thinking I was way more spiritually advanced than the other people there. When we got to the end of the talk the speaker invited us all to stand. He then said, "Put your hands out those who want to receive the Spirit." So I held my hands out. He then invited the Holy Spirit to come. Some people started singing in tongues and suddenly I started singing in tongues. I felt like a bird. I felt like this music was coming out of my mouth. It just happened. It felt like this beautiful voice came out—and I haven't got a beautiful voice. I felt flooded with warmth. I felt completely, completely at home. It felt like clear water was coming through me, pushing everything out of me. I started crying—sobbing and sobbing. I was still standing up but my whole body was shaking and my friend Caroline next to me was also shaking and that went on for quite a while. We were both sobbing.

After that we then both started hugging each other. We were crying and then we started laughing. That night after the session there was a disco and I was boogieing on the dance floor and thinking, *There's more to all this than I first thought . . .* I had a dream that night. There was a plant that kept floating up to the sky and the roots were all dangling and I kept trying to press the roots into the ground but it kept floating off again.

The next day we all regrouped in the main hall and there was a reading from Ephesians. It talked about Jesus being soil that we need to plant our roots in and then about how wide, how deep is God's love for us in Christ. I'd told Caroline about my dream and she turned to me and said, "That's what your dream meant last night."

I'd been trying to keep the plant in the soil and it kept rising up. I realized I needed Jesus to keep me planted in reality and help me deal with the world. I said a prayer, "Lord, forgive me for all the things I've done. I'm sorry for the things I've done in my past. I offer myself to you." I meant it. The weekend was amazing. I still had lots of questions but I got into the course more after that.

A good few weeks after the Alpha course had ended I started drifting back into thinking, *Oh well, I don't really need to become a Christian.* I then happened to speak to someone in the twelve-step program who was a

Christian and they said, "How's it going, becoming a Christian?"
I said, "Well, you know I don't really know if I'm supposed to
become a Christian or not." They said, "Well, just keep praying and
asking God." I said, "Oh I've been doing that." Then I remembered
that I'd had this little leaflet come through the door, which said, "God
will help you . . . Jesus is God's way. The Bible says in John 3:16–17:
'For God so loved the world that he gave his one and only Son, that
whoever believes in him shall not perish but have eternal life. For God
did not send his Son into the world to condemn the world, but to save
the world through him.' " And I told her this.

She then said, "Oh, my father died recently, we had his funeral last
week and that was the reading." She then said, "God sometimes speaks
to us through these coincidences."

The following day when I opened my Bible I happened to open it up
at John 3:16. I had randomly put the leaflet in my Bible as a bookmark
but I had put it on exactly the same page. I was like, "Okay. That's too
weird."

I went to church the next day and the reading was also the same
reading. I thought, *God is definitely trying to tell me something* so I joined
a pastorate [mid-week group]. After that I kept praying to Jesus to
show me the right way and basically my relationship with Jesus has
just been growing since then. I definitely had a relationship with God
before but now it's more intensified with Jesus. It's like the road that
I'm on, there's more light.

I read the Bible, but I still don't understand even 5 per cent of it but
I just keep reading. I've read the New Testament and now I'm reading
the Old Testament. In January 2003, I got baptized and I would say that
was when I properly became a Christian. I had been going to HTB for
six months and knew how much it was changing my life. I thought I
had to make a commitment. When I think of my past now I think it's all
quite dark. I don't know what the future holds, but I have God to help
me.

*After becoming a Christian, Donna Matthews returned to college to study for a BA in
Music. As a longstanding member of Ichthus Christian Fellowship, South London, she
recently completed the church's one-year leadership program. She is currently working
as a volunteer with people recovering from addiction.*

CHAPTER 9

PASTORAL CARE

The first words of Jesus to Peter (in Mark's Gospel) were: "Come, follow me . . . and I will send you out to fish for people" (Mark 1:17). In His last conversation with Peter (in John's Gospel) Jesus repeated, "Follow me!" (John 21:19) and urged Peter to feed and take care of the sheep and the lambs. The first priority is our relationship with Jesus. The second is our relationship with others.

In this last recorded conversation with Jesus on earth, Peter tells Jesus three times that he loves Him. Each time Jesus' response is to tell Peter to look after other people. If we love Jesus, we will make this a high priority in our lives. Indeed, it is part of following Jesus' example. He had compassion on people and once compared His longing to care for them and look after them to a hen with her chicks (Luke 13:34).

King David was a man who had experience of pastoral care as a shepherd tending sheep and also in the sense of being a shepherd of God's people. The psalmist says that "David shepherded them with integrity of heart; with skilful hands he led them" (Psalm 78:72). Pastoral care involves our *hearts* and our *hands*. We must have an integrity of heart: our love for people and our friendship with them must be genuine. There must be no false pretense. This love needs to be combined with "skillful hands." There are skills which we can learn. Obviously in a short chapter we cannot look at all the skills of pastoral care but I want to mention some of the general principles involved in this area.

The apostle Paul wrote: "He is the one we proclaim, admonishing and teaching everyone with all wisdom, so that we may present everyone fully mature in Christ. To this end I strenuously contend with all the energy Christ so powerfully works in me" (Colossians 1:28–29).

Aims

Paul's aim was to "present everyone fully mature in Christ" (v. 28). Some versions translate the word for mature as perfect. Perfection is not something we can reach in this life, but it is possible to become mature. Three vital points emerge from this verse.

First, Paul's concern is for *everyone*. A good pastor will not want to lose any of the sheep. The aim on Alpha is that every single person should be looked after, which is why each group has two main hosts and two helpers. The idea is that one of the hosts or helpers should take responsibility for each of the members in the group. It is a flexible and very relaxed system but the clear aim is that everyone on the course should receive care and prayer.

This system of one-on-one care is perhaps the most crucial aspect of Alpha. For myself, I owe so much to the man who helped me on an individual basis, early on in my Christian life. He sacrificed his time to answer my questions, explain the Christian faith to me, and to give me advice, guidance, and friendship. It was always fun to be with him: indeed, it was the highlight of my week as he helped me to lay the foundations of my Christian life.

Care like this is much more likely to meet people's needs. Preaching and teaching are inevitably like throwing a bucket of water over empty bottles, whereas one-on-one pastoral care is like filling each bottle individually from the tap. Not only is it the most effective method, it is also a form of Christian service in which everyone can take part as it does not require great speaking or leadership gifts.

Juan Carlos Ortiz tells the story of meeting an old lady in his native Argentina, who introduced him to a young girl who was one of her great-grandchildren. She went on to tell him that she had six children and thirty-six grandchildren. Her family was impressive in number and among her grandchildren were many well-educated and professional people. Ortiz asked her, "How did you manage to produce such a large, well-fed, well-dressed, well-educated, extended family?" She replied, "I didn't. I just took care of the six and each of them took care of their six."[1]

Preachers can overestimate the amount of truth that is assimilated between the pulpit and the pew. Bill Hybels and Don Cousins, leaders of the 20,000-strong Willow Creek Community Church near Chicago, have spoken about their experiences of coming to realize that sermons in and of themselves do not prepare people to live effective Christian lives. Hybels states that every major strategic step or decision he has made was inspired and encouraged by someone three feet from him and not in a crowd of a thousand people. "Truth applied across a table" has been a key to his own personal growth.

Second, our aim in this one-on-one pastoral care is *spiritual maturity*. Of course, this cannot happen overnight or even during a ten-week course. The hosts' and helpers' aim is to assist people through the early stages and then integrate them into a group within the life of the church, where they can grow and mature further.

The groups on Alpha are arranged, right from the start, with this express aim. That is why, ideally, the team in each small group should come from the same home group and at least one of the hosts or helpers should go with the group back to that home group and help introduce and integrate the new members.

Third, Paul's aim is maturity *in Christ*. We do not want to attach people to ourselves but to Christ. Good parents encourage independence in their children. They begin by feeding their children but teach them, as soon as possible, to feed themselves. We need to beware of any unhealthy dependence on us and help people to become dependent on Christ.

Our aim is that every person who comes to Alpha should come to spiritual maturity in Christ. In practice, of course, a number of people do drop out, as we saw in Chapter 5. But as in the parable of the sower, those for whom the seed falls on good soil, "hear the word, accept it, and produce a crop—thirty, sixty or even a hundred times what was sown" (Mark 4:20).

Method

Paul's method was to proclaim Christ. He wrote, "He is the one we proclaim, admonishing and teaching everyone with all wisdom" (Colossians 1:28). Jesus Christ is the key to spiritual maturity. We grow in maturity as our knowledge of Him and intimacy with Him grow.

Many of those who come to Alpha are not yet Christians. The aim is to lead them to Christ. They may give their lives to Christ during one of the main sessions or they may do it on their own. But every host and helper should know how to lead someone into a relationship with Christ. *Why Jesus?* is the booklet we use on Alpha as a resource in this area. I use it myself when explaining the Christian faith to those who are not Christians and then I encourage them to pray the prayer in the back of the booklet. Sometimes they will want to pray it on their own, but more often they would prefer to pray it out loud with someone.

Once people have come to Christ, it is vital to encourage them to grow in that relationship. Bible reading and prayer are the keys to this. We need to help them with reading the Bible and advise them as to how they might pray on their own. We can give practical advice about which translation of the Bible might be appropriate to buy and guide them towards some suitable Bible reading notes. And it is good to explain that Bible reading is not an end in itself but a means of experiencing a relationship with Jesus Christ (John 5:39–40).

As well as the Bible, Christian books can be a great help. We encourage people to read a balanced diet of doctrinal, biographical, and devotional books. Some are not great readers and prefer to listen to the Alpha talks and other subjects online, or on CD. We find many people enjoy listening to them in the car or when working around the home and this reinforces their faith.

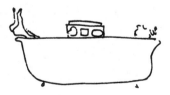

In order to become mature in Christ, people need to grow in their relationships within the body of Christ. The small group is the ideal place to start developing such friendships. As weekly meetings proceed, friendships grow quite naturally. We can encourage the process by acting as a catalyst for discussion in the early stages, when people don't know each other well. Later, if they start coming to church, it can help if group members arrange to meet and sit together. If any of them live near each other, giving rides encourages both the person who is giving the ride and the person who is receiving it, to come regularly.

Attitude

In helping people on Alpha to grow into maturity in Christ, we have found three principles to be of great importance:

Encouragement

In his early Christian life, Paul was much encouraged by Barnabas. He in turn became a great encourager (Acts 16:40; 20:1–2). He also wrote urging Christians to "encourage one another and build each other up" (1 Thessalonians 5:11). In the world there is so much negative criticism, leading all too often to insecurity and timidity. People shrivel up emotionally in an atmosphere of criticism and they thrive in an atmosphere of love and encouragement. We need to express warmth and responsiveness to those who are searching or are new Christians.

Listening

James writes, "Everyone should be quick to listen, slow to speak . . ." (James 1:19). It is the task of the team on Alpha to draw out the guests and listen to them. We should take a genuine interest in them and encourage them to speak about themselves. If guests have ideas that are contrary to the Christian faith, we should not be quick to correct them. First, we need to listen, to try to understand where the other person is coming from and to show respect for people even if we disagree totally with their ideas. If they reach a point where they are interested and intrigued enough to ask us what we think, they will pay far more attention to what we have to say.

Peacemaking

Jesus said, "Blessed are the peacemakers" (Matthew 5:9). It is important for the team on Alpha to be gracious and courteous and to avoid getting involved in arguments. On the whole, people will not be convinced if they get involved in an argument, especially if it is in front of others in the group. They tend to dig in their heels, which makes it harder for them to give up their position later if they wish to do so. It is easy to win an argument and lose a person. If there is an argument brewing, the host should try to reconcile differences and relieve tension, diplomatically exploring reasons for the differences. Usually there will be an element of truth in both points of view and the host can say, "Isn't it a bit of both? Fred is right in saying . . . and George is right in saying . . ." Then both Fred and George feel affirmed and the argument is over. Obviously, truth is what matters but the truth needs to be spoken in love and we need to be careful that "speaking the truth" is not an excuse for a personality clash, an expression of anger, or a wrong exertion of authority.

Commitment

Paul says, "To this end I strenuously contend with all the energy Christ so powerfully works in me" (Colossians 1:29). In Paul's pastoral care there was a balance between God's grace and his own responsibility. Our pastoral care should express the same balance. There is an element of "toiling" and "striving" involved in all effective Christian ministry.

Being on the team on Alpha involves a great deal of hard work. It requires a high level of commitment. Guests on Alpha are unlikely to reach a higher level of commitment than that of the hosts and helpers in their group. If the team does not attend regularly, those on Alpha are unlikely to do so. I ask hosts and helpers to write in their calendars all the evenings of the training course, as well as the ten Wednesdays of the course, the dinner at the end and the weekend. Of course, occasions will arise when they are unable to attend, because they are traveling or required to work or ill. But I ask them to give it the same priority they would give to their job.

This commitment is necessary because there are times when it will be a real effort to get there and talk to people sometimes until quite late at night. It requires an effort to talk to new people, rather than talking to friends. I ask people to pray and prepare beforehand so that when they are there they can concentrate all their efforts on the guests. This kind of effort makes for a very long evening.

Most important of all, helping on Alpha involves a commitment to pray. We ask the team to come to the prayer meeting at 6:30 P.M. every Wednesday, if they can possibly get away from work by then. We also ask them to commit themselves to praying regularly for every aspect of Alpha: the worship, talks, ministry, and administration, as well as praying daily, if they can, for the individual members of their group.

The other side of our responsibility is God's grace. We do not "strenuously contend" on our own. We do it "with the energy Christ so powerfully works" in us (Colossians 1:29). We need His help and His power for every task. When the disciples chose people to wait on tables they chose those who were "full of the Spirit and wisdom" (Acts 6:3).

I encourage all the team to receive from the Lord, both at the prayer meeting beforehand and during the main session, as they enter into the worship and listen to the talk. Even if they have heard the talk several times before they can pray that God will show them something new and relevant to their lives. All the time I encourage them to pray for God to fill them with His Spirit and empower them with all the gifts they need: evangelism, teaching, pastoring, and prophecy (the ability to hear what God is saying in a specific situation and pass it on to others).

It is this individual one-on-one pastoral care that is one of the most exciting aspects of Alpha. Members of the team often tell me thrilling stories about what has happened to an individual during the course. Not only has that individual's life been changed, but it has brought great blessing to the member of the team who befriended him or her. There is no greater joy than to lead someone to Christ and watch them begin to grow in the faith.

The nineteenth-century evangelist R. A. Torrey, writing on the subject of pastoral care, said he believed that when the membership of any local church exercises its responsibility and privilege in this matter, and each and every member of the church acts it out in the power of the Holy Spirit, "a great revival will be close at hand for the community in which that local church is located. [It] is a work that wins but little applause from men, but it accomplishes great things for God."[2]

THE STORY OF
JUDY CAHUSAC

CHAPTER 10

JUDY CAHUSAC

When her husband died in 1977, Judy Cahusac was left with two children under four years old and very little money to live on. Thirteen years later, and by then a successful businesswoman, she was persuaded to attend a service at Holy Trinity Brompton by her teenage son Bill . . .

I wasn't brought up in a Christian family at all. My father used to go to church, but he always left before the sermon. He just went for a couple of hymns and then left. At school we had something called Scripture but I don't remember learning anything. I came to London in 1963 after school and did a secretarial course, but my typing was awful. I went for lots of interviews but couldn't get a job. Then I spotted an advertisement in the *Evening Standard* for a secretarial job in a new nightclub that was starting in Soho. It was called The Establishment and turned out to be a new venture by comedians Peter Cook and Dudley Moore. They interviewed me and I got the job—chiefly, I suspect, because they never asked me if I could type. I was terribly excited.

The Establishment was London's first satirical nightclub and was the "in" place in the sixties. It lampooned all the people of the day and it was the beginning of the satire movement. I started off as the only employee. I worked from a dressing room at the back that had broken glass in the windows. The artists were always wandering in and practicing for their skits while I was trying to type the letters. It was only some time afterwards that Peter Cook and Dudley Moore discovered that their secretary couldn't type. They got a letter back from one person saying, "Your secretary's typing shows much dash and originality." Then the club started getting publicity and we had a huge deluge of people wanting membership. It was a really happening place. People used to book up months ahead to get in there and everybody came. *Beyond the Fringe*—Peter Cook and Dudley Moore's show—was on at the Fortune Theatre and the club typified London in the sixties. We would have David Frost calling to ask for a table and I would say, "No. We are full tonight, David!"

Throughout that time, I was leading a very nonChristian life. I lived in a flat with a whole lot of girls and there were a lot of men around the place. To be young and in London in the sixties was great. It was minis and wild and anything goes. The club folded a couple of years later. I kept in touch with Peter and Dudley for a while but they went off to New York with *Beyond the Fringe* and I moved on as well. I had a boyfriend whose mother worked for a recruitment agency, which seemed a good next step to me because you didn't have to type. I got a job with a small company with a staff of around ten people. While I was working there, I met Christopher, my husband, who was then married and in the process of a divorce. He owned the company. After a couple of years, we started living together and we were married in London in 1969. Four years after that, in 1973, we had Bill. Two years later George was born.

When George was one year old Chris began to develop pains in his chest and back. He also had a bad cough. He didn't feel great but he wasn't in agony. He went to one doctor who told him he had pinched a nerve in his back. Later, he went to another doctor who sent him to have tests done. In the hospital, they discovered his lung was full of fluid, so they kept him in to remove it. I was in the room with him watching as a doctor removed the fluid from his lung when the consultant came in and asked if he could have a word with me. He took me into another room and said, "I am afraid your husband is dying. He has got between six months and a year to live." He said he was sorry but there was nothing he could do. I was dumbstruck. I said, "Don't tell him," because I knew that he couldn't cope with it. The business was going through a difficult time and financially things were very difficult.

The doctor said, "We are not in the business of lying."

I said, "Well it is better not to tell him now."

Then I had to go back and have a conversation with him as if nothing had happened. It was awful. I told a couple of friends but I didn't tell him because he was so worried that the business was going badly and the children were tiny.

Throughout the next few weeks, I was thinking, *What am I going to do? How am I going to survive?* I also thought, *How am I going to stop him finding out,* because he was feeling progressively worse. Three months later he had an appointment with the doctor and the consultant broke the news to him. He called me at work and said, "They have told me that I have got up to a year to live." They just told him and then went out to lunch and left him. It was a very difficult time. Nobody said to either of us, "Do you want to come and talk to us?" or "Can we help?" There was no support or counseling for me and, worse, nothing for Christopher. He went through what I now have discovered are the fairly classic reactions of not accepting it, being angry and then accepting it.

I worked throughout this time because Christopher had sold the business by now to pay off its debts. We had no money and we had a girl to look after the children. Christopher got worse and worse. He was in and out of hospital quite a lot. As he became more and more ill, he was anxious to stay at home. Fortunately we had medical insurance so we were able to have nurses to care for him. It was awful to watch him deteriorate. Towards the end, I was also very ill. I had quinsy—which is a very rare abscess under your tonsils—and both children had chickenpox.

Although he was first cousin to David Watson [the late evangelist and author], Christopher wasn't a Christian at all. Then, one day, the doctor came to see him and said to me, "I think it will be days rather than weeks." The doctor left and I stayed sitting with Christopher who was sitting in a chair, very drugged up and wearing an oxygen mask. I was holding his hand when suddenly he took the mask off and stood up with a huge effort. Then he said, "There is someone at the door. Will you let them in?"

I said, "No, darling. It is the night nurse."

The night nurse had just arrived to relieve the day nurse.

He said, "No, no. There is someone at the door. Will you let them in?"

Then he just sat down gently and died—totally, totally peacefully. I watched it happen with complete amazement. I didn't know anything then about Jesus' famous words, "Behold, I stand at the door and

knock" but I definitely thought I was witnessing Christopher at the
gate of heaven. It was a great comfort to me. He died in 1977—almost
exactly a year after the consultant told me he was going to die. He was
forty-nine. I was thirty-three.

At the time, we lived in a rented flat and I had two children under
four. Christopher had sold the company. He had borrowed against his
life insurance, but I did get a lump sum of £20,000, which was quite a
lot more money then. Soon afterwards, the landlord decided to sell the
flats to the tenants, so I was able to buy the flat for £20,000—exactly the
amount that I had received from the life insurance. A year later, I was
able to sell it for £65,000, which enabled me to buy a house, the one
we live in now in Fulham. All the time I was still working for the same
company, although we no longer owned it. I had to pay someone to
look after my children, but it was the only way I could do it. Quite a lot
of my income went to that. It was very unsatisfactory.

Things went all right for a while but I felt that as I was effectively
running the company it would be fair if I had a share of the profits.
The owner said, "Okay. We will split it fifty/fifty." This worked
quite well until I began to suspect that he was doing better out of the
arrangement. I thought: "I have got two options. I have two small
children to support and a business partner who is making money off of
me. Either I can stay and put up with it or I can start on my own." So I
decided to start my own business. I just told him I was going.

He said, "I suppose I ought to tell you to leave immediately."

And I replied, "If I were you, I would."

So after having been there for twenty years, I put all my belongings
in a plastic bag and left. It was wonderful because it was just what I
had hoped would happen. Everyone said I was terribly brave to start
out on my own, but I didn't think of it as being brave until I sat there
with two empty books and no business. That was in 1986. I started
in a very tiny office just off Hanover Square on Princes Street. It was
just two rented rooms. One person who worked with me before came
with me. We were lucky because in the late eighties it was quite hard
not to make money. Although we couldn't directly approach any of
our clients, word got around quite quickly so people were coming to
us. Things were good. We specialized in secretarial jobs in the media,
television, and films. In 1989 we moved to Golden Square, just north of

Piccadilly Circus and very much in the center of the media area. All the time my children were growing up, which made me feel bad—worse now that I look back on it—because I could not be with them during the week much.

When Bill was approaching ten, I decided it would be better for the boys to go to boarding school if I could possibly afford it. Bringing up two energetic boys in a house in the middle of London was not easy. There was one school I liked and the headmaster was terribly kind and reduced the fees. He was wonderful to me. In many ways I felt bad sending them to boarding school, but in other ways I did feel that it was the best thing for them. In the holidays we always had a student to help and as I now had my own business, it was easier to take time off. Although it was difficult financially, it worked very well. Time went on and the business went well—until we were hit by the recession in the early nineties. I had four staff by then and it was tough. Then, in the summer of 1990, something happened that was to change our lives. A family named Barrett moved in two doors away from us.

It was a friendly street and there was a lot of curiosity about these new people moving in, who turned out to be a mother and four very attractive daughters. By now, Bill was sixteen and seemed to be at their front door all the time. "May I borrow a cup of sugar?"—anything! He used to come home in the evenings and go into the garden and stretch and jump up and down trying to look over the fence. Then he would say, "I think I am just going to go for a breath of fresh air"—and he would walk up and down outside their house. This happened so often that we came to call them the "fresh airs."

One Sunday they invited Bill to their church, Holy Trinity Brompton, and he accepted at once. He changed into his school suit and tie and went off. When he came back, he said, "Mom, it's brilliant. It's really good fun and they have really good music. You should go. They're nearly all young but a few of them are as old as you."

Later, Jenny Barrett, the girls' mother, invited me to a barbecue and said, "Why don't you come to church with us?" It was a Sunday afternoon and so we all went to the 6:30 P.M. evening service. The thing that impressed me most was the number of young people and the enthusiasm. I also liked the music. Bill became more and more involved with the church and I started going a couple of times a month in the evenings. Jenny would knock on the door and say, "Do you want to come this evening?" It wasn't a priority. I went to the carol service and the preacher invited members of the congregation to pray a prayer inviting Jesus into their lives. I remember praying the prayer and thinking, *Well, that probably doesn't mean very much.*

Later, I heard an interview with somebody in church who had attended a course called Alpha. The person being interviewed made it sound like good fun so I thought I would go and see what it was like. I went to the first night and really enjoyed it so I started going back. At that time, business was particularly badly hit by the recession and my accountant was telling me to lay off two members of my staff—but I couldn't because they had been with me for so long and had worked so hard. I mentioned this to my group leader in a chatty way over supper and later, during the small group session, she suggested that we pray for this. I said, "We can't pray for that. It's about money." I thought you could only pray for the Queen and peace and that sort of thing. The leader said, "Of course you can. You are not asking to be rich. You are asking for daily bread and you are also praying for these people." So we did pray and I was really touched.

The following week, the business got comparatively much, much better. I went back and everyone asked how things were. I said, "We have had a really good week," and the leader said, "There you are! That is an answer to prayer."

I enjoyed the Alpha weekend and then, some weeks after that, came the evening on healing. Towards the end of the evening, people began giving these "words of knowledge" about people who were ill. It was all completely new to me. Then they mentioned an injured right shoulder. As it happened, I had injured my shoulder about two years before and it still wasn't right. I couldn't lift my arm much higher than the horizontal and it didn't have the full range of movement. The moment I heard it, I knew I had to respond. There was no doubt in my mind. When I went forward, two people prayed for it to get better. After a while, they stopped and asked if it was any better. I remember swinging it round and round and being amazed that I could do it. It was completely healed. Then I thought, *Well this has got to be for real.* That was the moment that Jesus became real to me and I asked him into my life. I remember saying, "Thank You, Jesus, for healing me and I am sorry I didn't believe all the other things that You were doing. Now I know that You were there and thank You for being so patient."

I realized that I had been denying Jesus. I thought of all the things that had happened that I had probably thought were coincidences: Christopher's last words, the business turning round, other little things. At this time I was in a long-term relationship. Once I became a Christian, I knew that I had to end this—something that I would have found very difficult even six months before. I discussed it with my Alpha leader, who was very supportive and prayed for me. I was able to finish the relationship in a way that I would not have thought possible and we have been able to remain friends. I finished Alpha and got more and more involved in the church. I asked to help on the next course and then went on to help with about eight or ten more.

Bill, who had also become a Christian, was thrilled to bits. My other son, George, thought we were both crazy. He said it was like living in the Vatican! I felt I had so much to learn. I was like blotting paper, longing to catch up on all the years that I had missed out on. I started reading the Bible. It was hard because I had a very busy life and a fairly tight routine. To find time to do that was difficult and I didn't probably do it as often as I should at first.

I now think of Jesus with such love and such compassion. He represents such all-embracing, unreserved love. I suppose that if you have got children it is easier to understand that type of love. He is always there. I think now that I am happier in this stage of my life than I ever have been.

I wish I had been a Christian when Christopher died. I think I would have coped with it much better. I would have brought the boys up in a much more caring way—and I also would have had prayer support around me. I now think that God has been guiding me through my life without me even knowing it. I have no doubt that Christopher is in heaven—and I am so grateful for those last words of his. And I believe God helped me get away from the business that wasn't working and set out on my own. It was a completely crazy thing to do in retrospect—to walk away from a job that paid me a reasonable salary when I had two small boys completely dependent on me and a mortgage to pay. It could easily have failed. I am quite sure God was there looking after me and protecting the boys—for instance, the fact that the school reduced the fees and helped me to send the boys there. It was an extremely popular school with a very long waiting list and they needn't have done it. There was no doubt that God had a hand in that.

It is like meeting the Person who was looking after me all along.

Judy Cahusac is still an active member of Holy Trinity Brompton where she served on the church council for more than ten years. She sold her business in 2000 and now enjoys an active retirement.

CHAPTER 11

GIVING TALKS

Before I was a Christian, I was dragged to a talk that was one of a series in a church at Cambridge. I remember looking at the clock at the start, determined not to listen, and watching it all the way through the talk, amazed at how long it went on and how bored I was. Others seemed to be enjoying it and laughing. But I had told myself that I would not listen to a word of it.

When speaking to Christians it is not unreasonable to assume an interest. We expect from the congregation a hunger to find out more about the Christian faith, to try to understand doctrine and study the Bible. With those who are not Christians we cannot make any such assumptions. Rather, it is wise to assume they are asking, "Why should I listen?" and are challenging us to say something of interest to them.

We need to respond to this challenge. In the opening words, we have to tell them why they should listen. Truth in itself is not necessarily of interest. Truth is not the same as relevance. If we start by saying, "I want to expound the doctrine of justification by faith," then they are likely to fall asleep. On the whole, people are not interested in theology or historical background until they see its relevance. We must arouse their interest right at the beginning: the first few seconds are vital.

They have got to think, "This is interesting . . ." Like Jesus we need to begin with a need, a hurt, or something else of interest to the audience. Humor may be a way in, providing it leads us on to what we want to say. On the whole, people will listen to stories, whether they are humorous or serious. These should then lead into a subject

of relevance to the hearers: work, stress, loneliness, relationships, marriage, family life, suffering, death, guilt, or fear.

In this chapter I want to look at the whole subject of speaking to nonchurchgoers (e.g., those on Alpha) and in particular at giving an evangelistic talk (e.g., the Alpha dinner at the end of the course). I believe it is a skill that many people could acquire. The major requirement is a strong desire to communicate the good news about Jesus Christ. In preparing such a talk there are seven vital questions we need to ask. We will look at each of these in turn.

Is it biblical?

The Bishop of Wakefield, the Rt. Rev. Nigel McCulloch, described a sermon, which he heard while he was on vacation, as a "disgrace." "The preacher spoke long, but said little. There was no message. As I looked around at my fellow-worshipers I could see from the sleeping of the old and the fidgeting of the young that they, like me, were finding the sermon dull, uninspiring, and irrelevant. What a lost opportunity. In fact, what a disgrace." He did not reveal the content of the sermon, but he did observe that "the congregation does not want third-rate personal comments on public affairs but real preaching that brings the Bible to life . . . If St. Paul had been asked to advise the Church of England what to do in the Decade of Evangelism he would tell us what he told Timothy. In every pulpit, in every church, at every service 'preach the word'."[1] This does not mean that talks to people who don't go to church must necessarily be biblical exposition. Rather they should be based on biblical truth and have verses of the Bible woven into their fabric.

In giving an evangelistic talk at the Alpha dinner at the end of the course there are certain ingredients that I always try to include. Paul said that when he went to Corinth he "resolved to know nothing . . . except Jesus Christ and him crucified" (1 Corinthians 2:2). I try to ensure that every such talk is centered on Jesus. First, I say something about who He is, that Christianity is a historical faith based on the life, death, and resurrection of Jesus Christ, that the same Jesus is alive today and that it is possible for us to have a relationship with Him. Second, I include something on "him crucified." I speak of what Jesus did on the cross when He died for us and how He made it possible for our sins to be forgiven and our guilt to be removed. Third, I explain how someone can enter into a relationship with God, referring to repentance, faith, and receiving the Holy Spirit.

Is it good news?

In his first sermon, Jesus chose to preach on the text from the prophet Isaiah, "The Spirit of the Lord is on me, because he has anointed me to preach good news to the poor" (Luke 4:18). Jesus did not come to condemn the world but to save it. The gospel is good news in a world that is full of bad news. We should not simply make people feel guilty. We may need to talk about sin and guilt. But we do not want to leave people there. We are telling them about Jesus who frees us from sin, guilt, and evil. That is good news.

When Philip spoke to the Ethiopian eunuch he "told him the good news about Jesus" (Acts 8:35). I explain in the talk at the Alpha dinner that Jesus Christ meets our deepest needs. I know that those listening who are not yet Christians will be struggling somewhere deep down with a lack of ultimate meaning and purpose in their lives; they will have no satisfactory answer to the inevitable fact of death or the universal problem of guilt. In all probability they will also be aware of a sense of "cosmic loneliness," a sense of being in God's world without the God for and by whom they were made.

Aware of these needs, I try to show how Jesus dealt with our guilt on the cross, how He defeated death by His resurrection, how He made possible a relationship with God that gives meaning and purpose to life, and how He gives us His Holy Spirit so that we need never experience that cosmic loneliness. Of course, the good news of the kingdom of God includes far more than this. But in a twenty-minute talk at an Alpha dinner I stick to a few very basic parts of this good news. Whenever I have finished writing a talk I ask myself the question, "Is this talk good news?"

Is it interesting?

We live in an age of TV and computer games. People are not used to listening to long talks and it can be hard to retain their attention. Undiluted theology will not grip most people for very long. They prefer listening to stories and hearing how the point of them fits in with their lives. As a general rule, I find it helpful to follow the formula: point, illustration, application. If a talk has three points it will look something like this:

Introduction
i. Point
  • illustration
  • application
ii. Point
  • illustration
  • application
iii. Point
  • illustration
  • application
Conclusion

It is worthwhile collecting illustrations. They come primarily from our own experience, but they can also come from newspapers, radio, TV, movies, plays, books, and magazines. Of course, many of the best illustrations come from the Bible itself or from the natural world, and we need to think out carefully the applications for our listeners.

Is it persuasive?

Paul tried "to persuade" people (2 Corinthians 5:11). We need to work out what we are trying to achieve in a particular talk. For instance, are we trying to lead people to Christ, persuade them to start reading the Bible, or to pray? It is worth writing down at the top of the talk what our aim is. If we aim at nothing we are likely to hit nothing. If we aim at too much our efforts are likely to be dissipated. C. H. Spurgeon, the nineteenth-century preacher, said, "One tenpenny nail driven home and clenched will be more useful than a score of tin-tacks loosely fixed, to be pulled out again in an hour."[2]

Having established the aim, we need to ensure that every point is focused in that direction, like a tent supported from three or four different angles. We need to use every argument to appeal to the minds, hearts and wills of the hearers.

There must be an appeal to the mind. We must give people reasons for doing what we are urging them to do. Over the Alpha course we try to teach all the basic elements of the gospel. At an evangelistic Alpha dinner we try to teach the crucial elements of the good news.

If the talk were only appealing to the mind, it would be very dry. We need also to appeal to the heart. If, like me, you are British, you may find that hard. But people's emotions are involved as well. If it were purely an appeal to the emotions there would be a danger of emotionalism. Conversely, in appealing purely to the mind, we can stray into intellectualism.

Ultimately, if we are to persuade people to make a decision we need to appeal to their wills. In an evangelistic talk I try to drop a hint early on that there is a decision to be made, that there is no neutral ground, and there are no "don't knows" in the kingdom of God. I let them know what the options are. They can refuse Christ or accept Him or just put off the decision. All this must be done without any pressure. It is right to persuade but wrong to pressure.

Is it personal?

Bishop Phillips Brooks defined preaching as "the bringing of truth through personality."[3] Of course, the message we want to get across is objectively true and much of what we say will be proclaiming that truth. However, it is a great help for the hearers if we can illustrate these truths from our own experience. We need to be honest and real, not pretending that we are perfect or that we never struggle in any areas of our lives. This does not mean that we have to make embarrassing public confessions, but it is a help to acknowledge our own difficulties and failures. Stories told against ourselves can be both amusing and encouraging at the same time, provided they are set in a context that builds faith and is not purely negative. For example, I often tell stories about my early attempts at evangelism and the ridiculous things I did. I do it partly as a joke against myself, but also to assure people that we all make mistakes.

It is wise to talk generally in terms of "we" rather than "you." "You" can be very threatening and it suggests that we are somehow putting ourselves above our hearers. "We" is less threatening since it gives the impression that we are all in the same boat. "I" is the least threatening since it does not intimate that the hearers have the same problems: if it is used too frequently, however, the talk will appear self-centered. Generally I would suggest that "you" and "I" should be used sparingly. "You" is often effective at the end of a talk: "What do *you* make of the claims of Christ?" "Will you decide today . . .?"

Is it understandable?

It is no use giving the greatest talk in the world if no one can understand it. It is often said that we should never overestimate an audience's knowledge and never underestimate their intelligence. Because knowledge is limited we need to avoid jargon (which is familiar only to the "in" crowd) and technical terms such as "justification," "sanctification," "holiness," and "atonement" or any other word that is not used in everyday speech. The only case for using such words is if we explain simply what we mean by them.

The other side of the coin is that because most people's intelligence is reasonably high, there is very little that they will not understand provided it is clearly explained. Many theological books and talks are incomprehensible to most people: reasonably enough, if they are technical books for experts. However, I know for myself that if what I am saying gets very complicated, it is usually because I myself do not fully understand it. Albert Einstein once said, "You don't really understand something unless you can say it in a really simple way."

Certainly the teaching of Jesus was basically very simple. His economy in the Lord's Prayer, which comprises fifty-six words, is very favorable when compared to a recent EC regulation report on the sale of cabbages that totals 26,901 words!

Is it practical?

The Bible often exhorts us to be "doers" rather than just "hearers." James writes, "Do not merely listen to the word and so deceive yourselves. Do what it says" (James 1:22). Jesus Himself said that what distinguished the wise man (who built his house upon a rock) from the foolish man (who built his house on sand) was that the wise man put into practice what he heard (Matthew 7:24), whereas the foolish man did not.

If we are to help people put into practice what they hear, then we need to be very practical. We need to show them how they can do what we are talking about. In an evangelistic talk we should explain carefully what a person needs to do if they want to give their life to Christ. The vital elements in the New Testament response seem to be repentance, faith, and receiving the Holy Spirit. I explain these using the words sorry, thank you, and please.

I explain repentance in terms of asking forgiveness for the past and turning away from everything we know to be wrong (that is "sorry"). I explain faith as putting our trust in what Jesus did for us on the cross ("thank you") and I explain receiving the Spirit in terms of asking Him into our lives ("please"). Then I pray a prayer along the lines of the one in the booklet *Why Jesus?* and make it possible for them to pray that prayer in their hearts along with me.

Finally, it is good to remember that it is more important to prepare ourselves than to be prepared in the technique of giving talks. Billy Graham, speaking to 600 clergy in London in November 1979, said that if he had his ministry all over again he would make two changes. The audience looked rather startled. What could he mean? He said he would study three times as much as he had and he would give himself more to prayer. He quoted Dr. Donald Gray Barnhouse, who said, "If I had only three years to serve the Lord, I would spend two of them studying and preparing."

THE STORY OF
PETE DOBBS

CHAPTER 12

PETE DOBBS

Pete Dobbs, of Battersea, south London, enjoyed his reputation as a violent man. He took part in racist attacks, and was once hired to kill a man. Here he describes how a series of extraordinary events changed his life:

I've been to Chelsea Football (soccer) Club all my life. My dad took me first, just the once, when I was about five and after that I used to go with a friend. It was all terraces then, no seats, and I used to stand in The Shed. I didn't like school and used to skip classes—for weeks and weeks sometimes. I used to intercept the letters that they sent to my house so my mother never got them.

It was only after my dad died of a heart attack when I was fifteen that my mom explained to me that he had another home where he lived. He had a wife and would go home to her every night after I went to bed. When he died my mom and I went to where his wife lived to pay our condolences.

Soon after that I met Maureen, a girl my age, and I moved in with her and her family. My mom wasn't happy about it but I got along great with Maureen's parents. When I was seventeen we had a child, David, and we got our own place, a one-bedroom flat on the Mozart Estate in West London. It was quite a notorious neighborhood full of bad people, drugs, guns—the usual stuff.

Soon I started getting into fights at the soccer games. The head of Chelsea soccer violence then was a one-armed fellow named Babs who was known as the hard man of Chelsea. We'd fight against West Ham, Millwall, Cardiff—it didn't matter who it was. We'd meet up on a bit of wasteland or down a side street. Sometimes we'd go into a pub and smash it up—picking up chairs, ramming them through the windows, just causing trouble, until we got dispersed by the police.

I first got a motorcycle when I was about fourteen and my first car at sixteen. I was pulled over a few times as a youth without a license and insurance. I'd be given seven days to produce my documents but nothing happened when I failed to produce them. After leaving school I became an apprentice bricklayer for Southwark Council. It was a four-year apprenticeship but I did it in three years because my grades were good. I've always been good at that kind of stuff.

I started hanging around with the National Front when I was eighteen. I used to go on some marches. Sometimes a group of guys and I would go up Southall and abuse the foreigners—waving cricket bats, smacking a few about, picking on them randomly, beating them up. I became very aggressive. If a foreigner looked at me I might go over and say, "Who the ****ing hell do you think you're looking at?" and start pounding on him. Sometimes they'd get badly hurt. I don't think I've ever killed anybody, but I've certainly been steamed up and kicked them in the head, and stuff like that.

I started to go everywhere with the soccer matches. I've been hurt a few times, kicked to pieces, stamped on, punched. Once they whacked me in the kneecap with a baseball bat and I was in a wheelchair for six weeks. Once, when I was on my motorcycle, a guy cut me off along the Blackwall Tunnel. There's a side road to Hackney, with a concrete wall between the side road and the main road. After he cut me off I parked on the hard shoulder, got off my bike, then walked round the traffic median to where he was stuck in traffic. I put my fist straight through his window. I punched him several times in the face and took his car keys, then jumped back on my bike and rode off with his keys and left him there.

During the day I'd be working as a bricklayer and in the evenings I wasn't very nice to Maureen. I'd never shout at her, argue with her, or raise my hand to her—I've never done that to a woman in my life—but I just had so much aggression, so much anger. I don't know why. I stayed with Maureen until I was twenty, but I couldn't give her the love she deserved, so I started not coming home. By then we had two sons—David and Peter. I disappeared from their lives when they were still very young. Basically, I deserted them. Later she married someone else and I got a letter asking if I'd mind her husband adopting the children. I signed the papers, thinking, *Well, let them have a more controlled life . . .*

I ventured back down to New Cross and got to know a particular family there. One of the men in this family was a couple of years older

than me and he used to do burglaries and stuff like that. I went on a
couple of burglaries with him until one of his friends got caught for
something and snitched on us. We went to prison for nine months. I
spent my twenty-first birthday in jail but it didn't bother me.

After I came out I got back into work—and worked hard. I was
money motivated. I was a very good bricklayer, I was good at my trade
and I brought in the money. In the eighties there was a lot of money
in building, and we'd have a fairly new car every three years, two
vacations a year—one abroad, one at home. But I still went to soccer
matches, I couldn't pack that up. I still had a lot of rage and anger. I
was so very bitter. Someone would only have to say something and I'd
roar and bark at them, big time. People were frightened of me.

I then met a girl named Karen and we had two boys—Lee and Don.
Because I'd already lost my first two I didn't want to lose these ones.
She wanted to get married but I said, "No, take it or leave it." I took my
sons to soccer games but they just weren't into it. Then my son became
a Manchester United (soccer) fan and I said, "No, no, no, I'm not
having it—you ain't coming no more!" It wasn't a laughing matter—I
was horrified.

The Chelsea Headhunters appeared in the eighties. That was my
roughest period. Around that time I was approached by a family to pay
me some money to do away with somebody. The family was a very
well-known bad family in Southeast London and they knew about me.
They knew that if I was going to do something I would do it, I would
never back down. So they offered me an amount of money and I agreed
to do it. I had the photograph and went to the pub where this guy was
supposed to be drinking, with a sawn-off shotgun under my coat. I sat
there and had a couple of drinks while I waited for him to come in, but
he never came. If he'd come I would've done him. I had no thought
about it at all. I would have waited until he'd gone out of the pub, then
I would've followed him out and done him—Bang. But he didn't come
so I returned the weapon to the family and we rearranged it for another
month later. Then two members of this family got caught for something
else and got long-term imprisonments at Belmarsh.

I wasn't really in that gangster world. I got my feet wet, but I wasn't
really in it. I got involved with buying and selling hash through the
family and used to go round to their house and have a smoke, but

that was about it. After about eleven years with Karen I went up to Manchester to work there. I would see Karen every weekend. There were six of us living in a big house in Manchester for two years, while we were building several projects.

Soon after I came back, Karen and I split up after she cheated on me. A friend phoned me at work to tell me she'd been sleeping with this Irish man. So I went round to the man's flat and smashed the door in. He was asleep and I dragged him out of bed and punched him until he was unconscious. Then I got a hammer and some six-inch nails out of my bag and I nailed his hands and feet to the floor. He woke up screaming. I told him, "If you don't leave now, you'll be dead." He went back to Ireland and never came back.

My elder brother David had come out of the army after about nine years. He had been in Ireland and got shot by the IRA so he had to come home. Then he had a brain hemorrhage and died. He was thirty-seven. I was devastated.

In about 1998, I met Mandy in the Asda parking garage. Her car had broken down and she asked me if I'd give her a jump-start. So I started her car up and offered to help fix it. Then she gave me her phone number and I called her up and went to see her. It was like love at first sight for me. It was the first time I can honestly say I felt love for a woman—proper love. After about four weeks I moved in with her. During the day I was still very loud and had a lot of anger and rage—but the minute I got home I was like a different man with her. She became pregnant and we had a little girl named Breeze. We also moved to Colchester and I started to forget my soccer days.

A couple of years later I proposed to her and she said yes. We got married on May 1, 2004. It was a civil wedding because she was divorced, so we couldn't get married in a church. Things were very happy.

Mandy had been a Christian before and she started going to the Salvation Army in Colchester. One Sunday every month the Salvation Army would have a feast, where anyone could come and eat. So I used to go along as I always loved my food. I only went for the food. I got to know the minister, John O'Driscoll, and he tried to persuade me to come to a service. At first I always refused but then I started to go to the Sunday service at 10:30 A.M. They'd have all these songs and I started joining in. My favorite song is Amazing Grace (because of the soccer terraces) so I soon got in with the flow of things. But I still never thought nothing of it.

Then one Sunday in March 2007 I was sitting listening to John's sermon and all of a sudden I had these emotions. I could feel all this stirring inside my body. I didn't know what it was and I didn't like it. Then all of a sudden it was as if somebody had literally put their hand inside my stomach, grabbed me round my spine and just pulled me up. I got up and went to the front of the building where they have a place called a "mercy seat" where you can kneel. I'd never knelt before. I knelt down and floods of tears started coming out. Then one of the Sally Army elders came over and started praying for me. All of a sudden I said, "Look, I've been such a bad man. I don't know why but I've been so bad." And I shouted it out in front of everybody—the whole church service stopped.

The elder who was praying for me said, "Give it to the Lord . . . He'll forgive you."

I said, "I can't be forgiven for some of the things I've done." At that point I stood up because I wanted to get out of the church. But as I stood it was as if Mike Tyson had hit me with a right hook—I went down like a sack of spuds.

After about five minutes I got up. I was still in floods of tears. I couldn't stop crying and I felt so bad in myself as a human being. I got some cuddles and a bit of reassurance from my wife, but I couldn't cope with that. I went home. For the first time in my life I felt sorry—I don't think I'd ever said sorry to anybody. For the first time I felt pain, sadness, happiness—emotions I never knew I had. And the whole congregation—about fifty of them—was watching all this. When Mandy and I got home I was in bits so she called up this soldier from the Salvation Army and said, "Look, Pete's really in a bad way and I don't know what to do." So I went over to him and he prayed over me.

He said, "Pete, you've been touched by the Spirit."

I said, "Why would He want to touch me? What have I ever done?'"

And he said, "Pete, just let it out . . . He has forgiven you." I started babbling to him and crying on his shoulder. It was amazing.

That evening when I watched *Crimewatch*, I saw how people had done bad things to other people and it had me in floods of tears again.

I didn't go to work for nearly a week because I was so confused. Unknown to me, my wife Mandy had already decided she'd had enough of me. I'd never paid her enough attention. So we split up. The Salvation Army were praying for our marriage but she was having none of it. She asked for a divorce shortly afterwards. That was really weird when I thought I was changing so much.

I was working in London at the time so John, the minister, said to me, "Go and see Major Alan Norton in London" (he's some top guy in the Salvation Army). So I went to him, told him my story, begged for forgiveness from the Lord, and on June 5—Pentecost 2007—he helped me to pray a prayer asking Jesus into my life. On that day my anger—including my road rage—and stress levels just went. I stopped smoking hash immediately—I used to smoke every evening. After that, he said, "Pete, what do you want to do with your life?" I said, "I want to do as much as I can for my Lord. If I can give, I'll give. If I can do, I will do. The old Pete Dobbs is dead. I'm a new guy now and I want to live my life right."

He said, "Pete, go to the Alpha course."

I didn't have a clue what Alpha was going to do for me. He said that on Alpha I could grow and find out what God wanted for my life. He directed me to this church called Holy Trinity Brompton and I went. But they were just finishing their summer course and I only got there for the last week. I looked around and I was amazed to see so many nice people in one place. I thought, "I really want this . . ." I was itching to get onto the course. The next course started in September 2007.

I started going to a Salvation Army men's group on Mondays. Then on Tuesdays I was going to prayer evenings and I couldn't get enough of it. Then that September I started going to Alpha on Wednesdays. After Nicky Gumbel's talk that first week, I was like, "Wow, this is amazing. I really love this." For week after week, I was on a constant buzz.

I missed three soccer games because of Alpha. In the old days I would never have missed a Chelsea match like that—never in a million years. Soccer had always been first in my life. Then I went on the Alpha weekend in Chichester. That was absolutely awesome. I was like a junkie—a junkie for the Lord! I didn't know what to expect from the weekend but you could feel an electrical charge in the atmosphere. I was praying all weekend.

All my old friends say, "Pete, you're a different person." They can see the difference in me, big time. I don't sit there staring at people with a look of aggression on my face. I don't rant, I don't rave, I don't shout at them. I still cheer in soccer games but I don't sing the bad songs any more.

My language has changed—it used to be, "F this, F that . . ."—especially in my work as a bricklayer foreman. But I don't swear any more and I don't abuse. If the guys who work for me slack I will have to fire them, but I won't need to abuse them.

I go to Tollington Park Church on Sunday mornings now and in the afternoon I go to Wandsworth Salvation Army.

I took a Tottenham (soccer team) fan to Chelsea recently. I would never have done that before. While we were at the match, I must have had six phone calls from friends saying, "Pete, I've just spotted you coming into Chelsea, what you doing?" And I'd say, "I'm with my friend, my Tottenham, Christian brother."

"Oh you wimp!" and they'd rib me up a bit. But I can take it. They all know I'm a Christian and they think it's awesome. They're impressed. Now I get nonChristian friends —sometimes violent people, sometimes old drug-dealers—calling me up and saying, "Pete, would you say a prayer for such and such . . .?"

Apparently the definition of a psychopath is somebody who has no remorse for what they do. And people called me a psychopath. I didn't have any remorse for any of the things I did. I could have killed someone . . . I know that I have definitely been angry enough to do that. Whether it was the Lord stopping me from going that little step further, I will never know.

Now I'm never alone. Jesus is there with me all the time. Sometimes on my way to work I talk to him on my bike—it could be any time. I feel so contented and so at peace. I've virtually lost everything that meant anything to me and yet I'm still smiling.

Some time after becoming a Christian I decided to look for my oldest sons—David and Peter—who I hadn't seen since they were small children. I went onto Friends Reunited and looked up their mom, Maureen, and emailed her. We met a couple of months later and she said, "You're a changed man . . . You seem to be really mellow now." Then David got in touch with me and after a few emails we decided to get together. We first met in a pub at Earl's Court and I apologized to him. Meeting him again was really awesome.

Not long ago a car ran over my motorbike. I was visiting my boys, Lee and Don, and I heard crunch, crunch, crunch—some car had run over my motorbike. So I went up to the car and this little man got out. He was shaking. Before becoming a Christian I would have dragged him out of the car and battered him. This time I said, "Are you all right, mate? Look, sit down, don't worry about it."

He went, "It's your bike . . ."

I said, "Just sit there and chill, relax, catch your breath, make sure you're feeling fine. It's just a bike, don't worry about it." Then my ex-partner, Karen, came out and asked, "What's the matter?" And I said, "He's run over my bike." And she said, "I never heard nothing . . ."

I said, "Well, you wouldn't, you were indoors . . ."

She went, "No, I didn't hear you shouting. I didn't hear you. Someone's run over your bike and you've not said nothing . . .!"

I said, "Well, it's only a bike—what's a bike?"

So my life's turned full circle and I'm just loving every minute of it. It feels like I'm a millionaire, it really does. I'd never read a Bible before becoming a Christian. Now I read a bit of the Bible every day. Finding the Lord was the best thing that ever happened to me.

Now I can sense love. Before I couldn't give it or receive it. Now there's floods of it. I'm in awe of it all—I can't believe how lucky I am.

Since becoming a Christian, Pete Dobbs has done volunteer work with the Salvation Army and Alpha for Prisons. He has also been to Africa, where he and a group of other volunteers helped to build a school. He has recently moved to the north of England. He says, "I thank God for knocking on my door and making me new."

CHAPTER 13

PRAYER MINISTRY

What makes Alpha so exciting is the work of the Holy Spirit among us. It is His activity that transforms the talks, the discussion groups, the Bible studies, pastoral care, administration, and every other aspect of Alpha. The word "ministry" is used in several different ways in the New Testament and in the church today. In one sense, ministry includes everything done in a church and every aspect of an Alpha course. John Wimber defined ministry as "meeting the needs of others on the basis of God's resources." The *New Bible Dictionary* points out, "In its earliest form the Christian ministry is charismatic, i.e., it is a spiritual gift or supernatural endowment, whose exercise witnesses to the presence of the Holy Spirit in the Church."[1] In this chapter, however, I am using a narrower sense of the word: when we specifically pray for others in the power of the Holy Spirit.

One of the most astonishing stories in the Old Testament is the account of Moses and the people of Israel crossing the Red Sea. When they came to the sea God said to Moses, "Raise your staff and stretch out your hand over the sea to divide the water so that the Israelites can go through the sea on dry ground" (Exodus 14:16). God was asking Moses to do his part while promising to do His own part, by dividing the sea. I wonder what went through Moses' mind at that moment. He would have felt like an idiot if he had stretched out his hand and God had not divided the sea. He may have thought it would have been much easier if God had just divided the sea without involving him. But as is often the case in the Bible, there is a cooperation between us and God. God allows us to be involved in His plans. We do our part and God does His. Our part is relatively simple. God's is not so easy.

Moses took a step of faith and "stretched out his hand" (Exodus 14:21). God responded and ". . . all that night the Lord drove the sea back with a strong east wind and turned it into dry land. The waters were divided, and the Israelites went through the sea on dry ground, with a wall of water on their right and on their left" (Exodus 14:21–22).

God has not changed. This story reminds us that when we do what He asks us to do, He does what He has promised to do. As we pray for others He sends His Holy Spirit to transform lives. This might be prayer for others to be filled with the Spirit, to receive some gift (e.g., the gift of tongues), or prayer for healing.

Prayer ministry values

The most fundamental thing here is to recognize that this is a ministry of the Holy Spirit. It is not our power but His. What God asked Moses to do was very simple; he did not have to shout or dance or leap about. Likewise, we encourage our hosts to be totally natural and simply to be themselves, to take a step of faith and stretch out their hands and ask God to send His Spirit. The rest is up to Him. Sometimes I look around while ministry is happening and see hosts or helpers stepping out in faith for the first time in this area. There is often an expression of astonishment, bewilderment, and joy on their faces as they see how God uses them.

Sometimes when we see the extraordinary work of the Spirit we may be tempted to look at the fruit rather than the vine. But we are to keep looking to Jesus. Jesus taught His disciples not to be sidetracked in any way from the most important issues. When the seventy-two returned joyfully from the places they had been sent to minister to and said, "Lord, even the demons submit to us in your name" (Luke 10:17), Jesus replied, "I saw Satan fall like lightning from heaven. I have given you authority to trample on snakes and scorpions and to overcome all the power of the enemy; nothing will harm you. However, do not rejoice that the spirits submit to you, but rejoice that your names are written in heaven" (Luke 10:18–20).

Second, and of equal importance, all prayer ministry must take place under the authority of the Bible. The Spirit of God and the written Word of God will never be in conflict. They complement each other. God will never do or say anything that is inconsistent with His revealed will and character in the Bible. Because the Word and the Spirit go hand in hand we encourage our hosts to be steeped in the biblical truths and promises as part of ministry. It is the truth that sets people free (John 8:32). I ask people to make sure they know where key passages are that relate to the kinds of needs that emerge as we pray for people. For example, some of the passages we often use are the following: Psalm 51 (repentance), Psalm 91 (fear), Philippians 4:6–7 (anxiety), Psalm 37:5 (guidance), 1 Corinthians 10:13 (temptation).

Our third main concern in prayer ministry is the dignity of the individual: if we love people we will show them respect. This means first that confidentiality is assured. If people tell us confidential matters about their lives they need to be assured it will go no further. It will not be "shared for prayer" or discussed at helpers' meetings. Next, we must affirm rather than condemn. We don't say, "It's your fault," if people are not healed, or suggest that it was because they did not have enough faith. Jesus never told individuals that it was their lack of faith that stopped them from being healed. Occasionally He upbraided His disciples for their lack of faith (and we may need to ask ourselves whether we lack faith) but He never condemned the sick person in this way. We should not place additional burdens on anyone, let alone those who are sick. If they are not healed we never suggest that they should believe that they are. Rather, we give them the freedom to come back and pray again. This kind of prayer should always be done in a low-key way and any super-spirituality and unnatural intensity should be avoided at all costs.

The fourth value is harmonious relationships. Jesus prayed for His disciples, "May they be brought to complete unity to let the world know that you sent me and have loved them even as you have loved me" (John 17:23). The unity of the people of God was a high priority on Jesus' agenda and it should be so on ours. A lack of unity, love, and forgiveness on the team hinders the work of the Spirit and is a terrible example to those on Alpha. It is vital that each group's hosts and helpers find time to pray together, as prayer is the most effective way of rooting out petty irritations. We make it a rule on Alpha never to criticize another denomination, another Christian church, or a Christian leader. We try to support and encourage one another constantly. I discourage anyone from making negative remarks about another team member, even as a joke. We are extremely careful during the entertainment on the weekend away not to allow any skits that have even a hint of cynicism or are in any way negative. This may seem excessive, but we have found in the past that even the most off-the-cuff comment can have a detrimental effect.

Our fifth value is the vital importance of the body of Christ. The Christian community is the place where long-term healing and spiritual growth take place under the protective umbrella of the authority of the church. Hence, we stress that each person should try to find a group where they can grow and develop. Hosts and helpers are responsible for helping each person under their care to find such a group.

A model for prayer ministry

As well as having values on which our ministry is based, it is important to have a model about which we are confident so that all the theory may be put into practice and not left simply as theory. Over the years on Alpha we have developed a model, which is not the only way nor even necessarily the best way but it is one that we have found God works through and is simple enough for anyone to use and to feel confident in doing so.

When we pray for individuals we do so ideally with a team of two or, at most, three. Sometimes, for example on the Sunday morning of the Alpha weekend, there are so many people who want to be prayed for that there are not enough hosts and helpers to go around. On these occasions we may only have one person praying for each individual. If this is the case, we make it an absolute rule that men should pray for men and women for women. Often during these times of prayer the Holy Spirit brings out aspects of people's lives that are very personal and intimate. Also, at these moments a very strong bond may be formed between the person praying and the one being prayed for, and if the person is of the opposite sex there is a danger of misunderstanding and a misreading of signals. If there is more than one person praying then at least one should be of the same sex as the person being prayed for.

At these prayer times one person should take the lead and should be seen to do so with the prayerful help of the others. If more than one person is attempting to lead there is a danger that signals will be confused. For example, it is not helpful if one is saying, "Hold on," and the other is saying, "Let go!"

As far as possible it is good to find a relaxed and private place to pray. If there are a lot of people in the room, it is important that others around cannot hear everything that is being said, to avoid embarrassment for the person receiving prayer. In other situations, I have sometimes seen the most inappropriate raising of voices and even shouting, to the intense discomfort of the person receiving prayer.

We usually begin by asking the person what they would like prayer for. We then take time to sort out difficulties in understanding, belief, and assurance. Often there is a need for repentance and forgiveness, both receiving forgiveness and forgiving others. Lack of repentance and forgiveness is a major stumbling block to the work of the Holy Spirit in our lives.

Sometimes at this point it becomes clear that the person is not yet a Christian. Each member of the team needs to be confident that they can lead someone to Christ. I would usually go through the booklet *Why Jesus?* briefly and then ask the person if they would like to pray the prayer in the back right then or whether they would rather go away and think about it (it is important always to give people an out that is equally acceptable so that they do not feel pressured into doing something for which they are not ready). If they say they would like to do so right then, I would pray for them briefly and then encourage them to read the prayer out loud, slowly and thoughtfully, adding anything they wish. After this I would pray another prayer for them asking the Spirit of God to come and fill them.

Others may already be Christians but have never really experienced God or the power of the Holy Spirit. We need to encourage them with truth through scriptural illustrations and promises. We need to deal with any difficulties they may have. They may say, "Am I quite ready?" to which the answer, in one sense, is that we will never be totally ready. Some say, "I'm unworthy," to which the answer is, "We are all unworthy. That is why Jesus died for us." Most often there is a feeling that it could "never happen to me." For example, they might want to receive the gift of tongues but say, "I could never speak in another language." Again, we need to raise faith by pointing to the promises of God (1 Corinthians 14:2, 4, 14; Matthew 7:11). One aspect of faith is taking a promise of God and daring to believe it.

As we pray for the person we stay facing them and, if they have no objection, we lay hands on them. Then, keeping our eyes open, we ask the Holy Spirit to come. We welcome Him when we see signs of His working and wait on God as we pray for further directions. It is important not to pray "around-the-world" prayers, i.e., going off in every conceivable direction because we are running out of things to pray. Rather, we should silently ask God what He wants to do or say, how He wants to encourage the person and what gifts He wants to impart.

On the Alpha weekend we often pray for people to receive the gift of tongues (see *Questions of Life*, pp. 144–151). This is not because it is the most important gift but because the Alpha course is a beginners' course and the gift of tongues is a beginners' gift. It is neither the mark of being a Christian, nor a necessary sign of being filled with the Spirit. The gift of tongues does not elevate you into a spiritual elite, nor is it indeed necessary to speak in tongues. However, both in the Bible and in experience it is often the first obviously supernatural gift of the Spirit that people receive. Our understanding of the New Testament is that it is available to all Christians and therefore we can pray with great confidence for them to receive.

The small group is the place to deal with people's fears and hesitations. I would ask those in the small group if anyone has had any experience in this area, good or bad. If they have, I ask them to speak about it. Usually there is someone (it might be a host or a helper) who speaks in tongues themselves and is able to explain what it is and what the benefits are.

When praying for people to receive the gift of tongues I have found the greatest barrier is a psychological one—making the first sound. Once a person has made the first sound the rest usually follows quite naturally. In order to help people to get over this barrier I explain this difficulty and suggest that they start by copying what I or one of the other pray-ers is saying. Then I start to speak in tongues slowly so that they can follow. Once they have made the first sound they are usually away praying in their own language. I encourage them to try and concentrate on their relationship with God and try, as far as possible, not to be self-conscious. Rather they should concentrate on praising God with the new language He has given to them.

After we have finished praying for a person to be filled with the Spirit, receive a gift, be healed, or whatever it is, we should ask what is happening and what they sense God is saying to them. We should encourage them to hold on to the promises of God, and warn them against possible increased temptation. We don't believe it is possible that "nothing has happened." They may not be aware especially at the time but when we ask the Spirit of God to come, He has promised to come. They may not know the difference until hours or even days later but something will have happened. We need to encourage them to keep in touch and to let us know how they are getting along. Of course, it is not a one-off experience; they need to go on being filled with the Spirit (Ephesians 5:18).

Opportunities for prayer ministry

Much of the prayer ministry takes place on the weekend away. The early part of the weekend is usually spent in raising faith and dealing with difficulties. On Friday night we have a very short talk on the Holy Spirit based on John 15:26. I try to keep this short and light-hearted as people are often exhausted after a busy week and a long journey.

On the Saturday morning we look at "Who is the Holy Spirit?" and "What Does the Holy Spirit Do?" (see *Questions of Life*, chapters 8 and 9). Then at 12 noon we go into the usual small groups and look at 1 Corinthians 12:4–11. This gives people an opportunity to discuss some of the most obviously supernatural gifts of the Spirit.

On Saturday afternoon there is an opportunity to ask for counseling with an experienced (though not professionally trained) counselor. We put up a list of the counselors and people can sign up for this if they have questions they want to ask, difficulties they would like help in thinking through, or if they would like to receive prayer for some area in their lives. During these sessions some give their lives to Christ, some are filled with the Spirit; others receive new gifts.

On the Saturday evening (at 5:00 P.M.) I speak on "How Can I be Filled with the Holy Spirit?" (chapter 10 in *Questions of Life*). At the end of the talk I explain that I am going to invite the Holy Spirit to come and fill those who would like to be filled and give the gift of tongues to those who would like to receive. I ask everyone to stand, to close their eyes, and to hold out their hands in front of them if they would like to receive. Our body language often expresses what we feel, and holding out our hands is what we do when we are about to receive a gift: thus it is a sign between the person and God that they would like to receive.

I then pray a prayer that others can echo in their hearts. It is a prayer of repentance, faith, and commitment to Jesus Christ. I then ask the Holy Spirit to come and fill all those who have invited Him into their lives. We then wait and watch as He comes and does what He wants to do. It is always different and always exciting to see God at work in our midst. Sometimes the manifestations of the Spirit are obvious. Some are so overwhelmed by the Holy Spirit they find it hard to remain standing. Others are so deeply moved by the love of God that tears run down their faces. Some are so filled with joy that they burst out laughing. For others there is no outward manifestation but a work of God in their hearts is bringing a sense of peace and a deep assurance of His presence and love. All should be encouraged, and no one should be made to feel guilty, second-rate, or rushed along against their will.

At the end of the course I send out questionnaires asking (a) whether people were Christians before the course and (b) how they would describe themselves now. If there is a change I ask when that change occurred. For many the decisive moment is the Saturday evening of the weekend. Here are five examples of how people at one Alpha weekend described their experiences:

– "After the talk about 'How can I be filled with the Holy Spirit?' we all stood up and the Holy Spirit came into the room. I knew that God was real so I asked Jesus into my heart and He's been there ever since . . . I have suddenly got a whole new outlook on life."

– The change had occurred "during the Saturday evening talks/ services. I was filled with the Holy Spirit. I felt a white sheet wipe me clean then a strong rush of light came through me from my waist and up out of my head—the feeling made me lift my arms in the air."

– "I had been a Christian in my head only. This changed on the Alpha weekend when God spoke to me personally. I asked Him for His Holy Spirit and the result was electrifying."

– Someone who had been involved in the New Age movement at the start of the course said that the change occurred on the Saturday evening when "the Spirit shook me from head to foot."

– "I had a phenomenal experience of the Holy Spirit cleansing me, freeing me, releasing my sins and loving me; giving me a fresh plateau, a new life. It was the 20th of February when I really started to *live!*"

After the Saturday evening we respond to God in songs of thanksgiving and praise. Sometimes we will sing in tongues. I explain that singing in tongues together is different from all speaking in tongues together. Speaking in tongues without interpretation is a private activity which should only be done on our own. Singing in tongues is a corporate activity of praise and worship to God, coordinated by the Spirit of God. On occasions, it has been one of the most beautiful and almost angelic sounds I have ever heard. It is also a golden opportunity for people to receive the gift of tongues as they begin to sing praises to God in the language He gives them.

We do not usually pray for individuals on the Saturday night unless they specifically ask for prayer (which some often do at this stage). Instead, after supper we have an evening of entertainment organized by someone on the team. This is a good time for people to relax and unwind by performing or watching. We invite participation by anyone who would like to contribute. It is usually a mixture of musical contributions, joke telling, and amusing skits. The quality is sometimes a little mixed, but it always involves lots of laughter. We try to ensure that the whole evening is as positive and upbuilding as possible.

On Sunday morning at 9:45 A.M. we meet in small groups briefly to make sure that everyone is happy and to discuss any difficulties or questions which may have arisen on the Saturday, and at 10:30 A.M. we have our informal communion service. We begin with praise and prayer. Then we have a talk on "How Can I Make the Most of the Rest of my Life?" (see *Questions of Life*, chapter 15). At the end I invite people to give every part of their lives to God, "to offer your bodies as living sacrifices" (Romans 12:1). This is the appropriate response to all that God has done for us. In some circles it would be described as a "wholeheartedness talk." It might be argued that this should come before the talk on being filled with the Spirit; that as we open all the doors of our house He fills each part with His Spirit. I am sure there is something in this, but the movement in Scripture is from Him to us. He blesses us out of sheer grace and mercy and we respond by giving ourselves to Him out of love. When we begin to understand and experience the love of God for us as we are filled with His Spirit, our only appropriate response is to give everything we have to Him.

After the talk, we greet one another with a sign of peace. At this stage we have a few moments' break and move around greeting one another and chatting briefly. By this time there is a lot to talk and laugh about and it is usually quite loud! After the peace we sing a song of praise. We have an offering that covers the cost of those who could not afford to pay for all or part of the weekend. One of the exciting things about these weekends is that we almost always end up with exactly the amount in the offering to cover those we have subsidized. People are learning right from the start that in the Christian family those who have more should help those who have less.

I then explain the communion service (along the lines of *Questions of Life*, pp. 206–207). This is a good opportunity to teach about the central service of the Christian faith. Many comment on the beautiful simplicity and unity in this, and some experience God's love for the first time as they relax and receive the bread and wine.

After the communion is over I invite people to stand and again ask the Holy Spirit to come and work among us. After waiting for a short time I ask members of the team to begin praying with those who would like prayer. At this stage it is important for each member of the team to have the courage and confidence to go and pray for those in their groups along the lines I have suggested earlier in this chapter. This prayer goes on for some time. I usually end the service with a song and the blessing at around 1:00 P.M., but prayer for some continues while the rest of us go to lunch.

After lunch, at 2:00 P.M., we gather for five minutes to give thanks to our hosts and deal with any final administrative matters. We arrange to meet at the evening service (for those who are able to come), and reserve all the front seats of the church for those who have been on the weekend. For many it is their first time in the church. There is always a sense of great excitement and celebration on these occasions. The ministry of the Spirit continues and some are filled with the Spirit and receive gifts during or after the evening service.

Another excellent opportunity for those on the course to learn about prayer ministry is the healing evening (*Questions of Life*, chapter 13), which occurs during week nine. The evening follows the normal pattern until the end of the talk. For smaller courses we recommend that you do not break into small groups after the talk, but rather stay together for a practical time of prayer ministry for healing. For larger courses it may be more manageable to do this in the small group context, where guests will have the opportunity to respond to a word of knowledge and receive prayer.

Before this time of prayer we explain what is going to happen—outlining the model of healing prayer that we follow (*Questions of Life*, pp. 192–193). We then explain that God sometimes gives words of knowledge (1 Corinthians 12:8), which build faith and point out whom God wants us to pray for specifically. We have found that people receive these words in various ways. Some may get a mental picture of the part of the body that God wants to heal. Some will merely receive an impression, and others may sense that they hear or see words. We have found that one of the most common ways we receive words of knowledge is by what we call "a sympathy pain": someone senses pain in their body, which they know is not really theirs.

Simon Dixon, who became our organist, had a stabbing pain when he moved or when he was touched around his jaw or neck. It had been very painful for a year and a half and he had been told it couldn't be cured. He had lots of medical tests, but the doctors did not know what was wrong. They thought it might be a brain tumor. He was finally diagnosed as having auricular neuralgia. He was on a lot of drugs and at times his vision was affected. A woman in our congregation named Emma had felt a pain in her jaw, which she thought must be a sympathy pain and therefore a word of knowledge. As a result, after prayer for healing, he was sufficiently cured to come off the drugs and after further prayer was totally healed. Since then he has been perfectly healthy.

At the end of this explanation we ask if anyone senses that they have any words of knowledge. Usually there are many—often received by those who are relatively new Christians who have never had the disadvantage of being told that God does not speak to His people today. They expect God to speak to them and He does. We write down all the words of knowledge. In the corporate setting we go through the list one by one, sometimes asking people to identify themselves (providing, of course, the condition described is not one likely to cause embarrassment), or on other occasions we simply ask all those who want to respond to stand at the same time. On larger courses, the guests are given the opportunity to respond and receive prayer within their small group.

Next, we ask one of those who have responded (if they are willing) to be prayed for. We then get two or three experienced people to pray for the person to provide a model of how to pray for healing. Whoever is leading the evening explains exactly what is happening.

Then we arrange for two or three people to pray for each of those who have responded to the words of knowledge. We try to get those who have had the particular words of knowledge to pray for those who responded to them. By this time almost everyone on the course is involved in the prayer ministry. If there are any not involved we suggest they join a group to watch and learn from what is going on.

It is very exciting to see those who have only recently come to Christ praying, often with great faith, for others in a similar position. We have seen some remarkable healings on these evenings and we nearly always see conversions as well. I remember the time a teenager named Bill brought his mother Judy on an Alpha course. She had enjoyed the course but was still quite sceptical about the healing evening. That night there was a word of knowledge for a shoulder injury. She responded and was healed. She said afterwards, "Many things had happened to me during Alpha that were answers to prayer, which I had tried to explain away as coincidences, but it was the healing that made me realize that I could no longer say it was a coincidence. I prayed in my heart and made a commitment." Since then she has been a helper on a number of Alpha courses, being increasingly involved in the organization and administration. Read Judy's full story in Chapter 10.

The ministry of the Spirit is crucial to Alpha—without it, it would not really be an Alpha course. We have found that time and again God has honored simple requests for Him to send His Spirit among us. Amazing and profound changes always occur in people's lives as a result. We are continuing to see people give their lives to Christ, be filled with the Spirit, get excited about Jesus, and bring their friends to the next course.

ALPHA TALK SCHEME

The fifteen talks that make up the Alpha course are:

1. Is There More to Life Than This?	Introductory session
2. Who Is Jesus?	Session 1
3. Why Did Jesus Die?	Session 2
4. How Can We Have Faith?	Session 3
5. Why and How Do I Pray?	Session 4
6. Why and How Should I Read the Bible?	Session 5
7. How Does God Guide Us?	Session 6
8. Who Is the Holy Spirit?	Weekend away talk 1
9. What Does the Holy Spirit Do?	Weekend away talk 2
10. How Can I Be Filled with the Holy Spirit?	Weekend away talk 3
11. How Can I Resist Evil?	Session 7
12. Why and How Should I Tell Others?	Session 8
13. Does God Heal Today?	Session 9
14. What About the Church?	Session 10
15. How Can I Make the Most of the Rest of My Life?	Weekend away talk 4

Talk 1 is given at the celebration dinner at the end of the course. Talks 8, 9, 10 and 15 are given at the weekend away. The best time for the weekend is halfway through the course, but the date is flexible. If it comes later then the talk scheme needs to be adjusted accordingly. Whenever the weekend falls it is helpful to give Talk 11, "How Can I Resist Evil?", directly afterwards even if it means the sequence of the talks changes slightly. This is because we have found this subject very relevant at this point.

ADMINISTRATION

On an Alpha course there is a lot of hard work behind the scenes and every job is vitally important. We aim to get everything 100 percent right. Guests who come on the course will see that every effort has been made and that everything is run in an efficient way.

Some of this chapter will only apply to larger courses, where the first thing the course leader should do is appoint a director.

Set a date

Make sure that your Alpha course does not overlap with anything that will keep people from coming, e.g., Christmas, Easter, and summer vacations. Remember to allow enough time for the dinner parties at the end of the course and the three training sessions. If you are doing a daytime Alpha (see Appendix C) then tie in your course with the school schedule and include vacation times during the appropriate dates. We suggest you do not book the weekend away over vacation times.

Prepare brochure/letter

Prepare a flyer with all the relevant details and feel free to reproduce the Alpha logo in accordance with the Alpha International brand guidelines. Alternatively, produce a simple letter that sets out all the dates with a tear-off slip at the bottom. It is also possible to purchase Alpha Invitations, which can be customized with your own course details.

Another effective way of advertising your course details or inviting potential guests to your course is via social networking sites such as Facebook and Twitter. These tend to work virally as people post information to their personal profiles and circulate the invitations among their own friends.

Next, contact the home group leaders of the church and ask them to suggest people whom they know who would be good Alpha hosts and helpers. It is vital to get the right people (see Chapters 3 and 5). It is important to emphasize commitment to the course, because if the hosts are not consistent in coming then there is no reason why anybody else should come either.

Emphasize that their commitment is not just for ten weeks but also for three training nights, social evenings with their group, follow-up after the course has finished, getting members into a home group, and integrating them into the church. Insist that all hosts and helpers come to the training sessions. If they are unable to come, ask them to watch the talk on DVD. Even if some of your team have helped on several Alpha courses, they should come to every training session of every course. Even if one of your hosts has been leading home groups for twenty years or so, stress that Alpha small groups are very different. Ask the hosts and helpers to commit themselves to pray for every member of their group.

Organizing a team

This can be a very long task, so allow plenty of time. Be firm with your team, emphasizing that everyone should be willing to do anything from hosting to cleaning-up.

Arrange groups primarily by age and think carefully about the dynamics of the group: the balance of characters, social backgrounds, professions, etc. It is also good to select a team from the same home group so that there can be continuity for the guests after the course, although this may not always work in practice. It is better to put together a team who will work well with one another. If you can, try to allocate a specific person in each group to look after the administration for their group, preferably someone who is gifted in that area and who can definitely come to the administration/prayer meetings every week.

Advertising

The most effective way of advertising an Alpha course is through the celebration dinner at the end of the course. This provides an opportunity for guests to invite their friends to see what they have been doing for the last ten weeks. (The dinner is discussed in more detail later on in this Appendix.)

The two Sundays prior to the beginning of the Alpha course should be designated "Alpha Sundays." At Holy Trinity Brompton the first Sunday is a regular service with a testimony and a slot advertising Alpha. The second Sunday is a guest service that is designed especially for church members to invite their friends and family. This service is low-key and the sermon is evangelistic and challenging. Again Alpha would be advertised and a testimony heard. Alpha brochures and complimentary copies of *Why Jesus?* are given to everyone at the end. An easily identifiable Alpha team is available afterwards to answer questions.

Suggested guest service timetable

6:30 P.M.	Welcome
6:35 P.M.	Praise and worship
6:50 P.M.	Prayers
6:55 P.M.	Description of Alpha and one or two testimonies from people who have just completed the last course. We would suggest that nothing else is promoted at this point.
7:05 P.M.	Hymn or song

7:10 P.M.	Reading
7:15 P.M.	Sermon
7:35 P.M.	Hymn or song
7:40 P.M.	Final prayer, blessing, and offer of one-to-one prayer ministry

Other churches have found that an advertisement in the parish magazine or on their church's website is helpful. Another idea is to send personal invitations to people in your area.

Placing guests in groups

Often you will have very little information about your guests. From the application form you may only have their name, address, telephone number, an idea of their age, and their handwriting!

Remember that these are individuals. At Holy Trinity Brompton we pray over almost every single application and ask for guidance. If someone is not happy in their group, they might well not come back, so it is very important to get it right. If you feel there is a genuine reason (e.g., a large age gap from the rest of the group) why someone should move to a different group, do it in the first week otherwise it is disruptive for those in the old group, as well as the new one.

If a guest is a friend of someone on the team, try to find out as much as possible about the guest, which will help you to put them in the right group. Quite often, it is better not to put the guest in the same group as their friend who is helping as they often feel inhibited and unable to ask questions. Always put married couples in the same group unless specifically requested not to. Aim to arrange to do this task a few days before the course starts. This will give you a chance to ensure any last-minute applications are on your list, allocated a group and will have a pre-printed label.

Venue

One of the features of Alpha is that the setting should be unchurchy. The ideal venue is a home, but when the church outgrows a home a venue with a welcoming atmosphere needs to be found. It can often be difficult to make a church hall look welcoming. Use standard lamps instead of overhead strip lighting; provide flowers; cover unattractive trestle tables; make sure that the room is warm but not stuffy; arrange the chairs so that guests can eat together in their groups. Make sure that there is good lighting on the speaker and that everyone is able to hear. This may involve arranging a PA system. Make sure that there is somewhere for people to leave their coats and a secure place for briefcases, bags, etc.

FIRST NIGHT

It is also useful to have signs for directions to restrooms, the booktable, and where groups are meeting—put up a map if necessary.

First night

Your welcoming team are going to be the first people your guests will see. Often they arrive with many preconceived ideas of what Christians are like, so when they are greeted by a "normal" person they are often surprised and it is very important that their first impression is a good one.

Your welcomers will need an alphabetical list of guests with the name of their group hosts and the group number. They will need to know how many men and how many women are in each group. This is helpful when unexpected guests arrive and need to be placed very quickly in a group. Welcomers should know who the group hosts and helpers are, and have to hand a list and a plan of where the groups are meeting.

At the end of the first evening of the course all the hosts and helpers should meet together to discuss and review the evening.

Name Tags

Every person should have a name tag with their name and group number on. (Ensure that the names are spelled correctly—accuracy is very important.) Set up a table with labels in alphabetical order and delegate one or two people to hand them out. Alternatively, provide a pack/folder with ready-made labels for each group host. Give team members a different colored name tag so that guests can know who they are and ask them any questions. Keep some spare name tags and a list of unexpected guests so that they have a pre-prepared label for the following week. We have found it useful to continue using name tags until week three.

Runners

Depending on the size and venue of your course you will know at what stage you will need runners. You will need to choose a team of runners (i.e., those who take the guests from the door to the group) who are headed up by a strong leader. Keep a team of runners for the first three weeks. Don't use group hosts as they will need to be in their groups to greet people. Again, remember that first impressions are important. The runner must be alert to remember the name, group number, and location of the group. The welcomer should introduce the guest to the runner who will take the guest to get a name tag and take them to their group and introduce them to their group hosts. Then they should return quickly to the main door. Obviously, welcomers and runners should be friendly, but not effusive, as this can overwhelm guests on the first night.

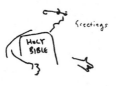

Address lists

We give each group a blank form for them to fill in names and addresses and contact telephone numbers. However, it must be stressed to all the guests that this is not so that they will be sent junk mail or be called on the telephone when they don't come back to the course. These lists are then typed up and one copy is returned to the group host, updated each week until the fourth week.

This is so that redos may be arranged and guests may be contacted if there is any problem. We do not give each member of the group a copy of the list—if they want to exchange addresses and telephone numbers this can be done within the group. If a guest calls the church office for a telephone number of another guest, we do not give details under any circumstances.

Booktable

There is a list of recommended books in the *Alpha Course Manual*. Ideally a booktable should be open for the whole evening (except during the talk). Ensure that audio recordings of the previous weeks' talks are available on CD so that anyone who missed a session can watch or listen to it later.

Treasurer

The treasurer will need to keep the overall accounts. He or she will also need to put out some bowls for dinner money and count it at the end of every evening. Furthermore, they will need to collect and count the weekend money and the celebration dinner money.

Worship leader

The worship leader needs to be responsible for any other musicians, the songbooks, all the sound equipment and perhaps also the taping of the talks, and will need to make sure that the weekend away has a worship leader.

Weekend organizer

Each group should fill in a form for the weekend, which should be circulated two or three weeks before the event. Include on the form details of the date, price, to whom checks should be made payable and children's rates. Ask for information regarding special diets, vegetarian meals, requests to share and late arrivals. Try to get people to arrange their own rides and transportation within the groups. Make sure that everyone has a map and a program for the weekend (see Chapter 3).

- Contact with the conference center about:
  sheets
  towels
  soap
  special diets
  bookshop—check that they are happy for you to take your   own stock
  communion wine/juice
  PA system
  recording equipment
  projector and screen
  sports facilities
  places for small groups to meet
- Arrange for a CPR-checked volunteer to look after any children (encourage people to bring their children if they would like to)
- Arrange for someone to organize entertainment on the Saturday evening
- Arrange for someone to organize sports, activities, or other events on Saturday afternoon
- Arrange for counselors for people to chat to on Saturday afternoon
- Remember to take a calculator
- Remember to take songbooks
- Remind guests to bring their *Alpha Course Manual* and their Bible and any sports equipment
- Take spare Bibles and manuals
- Remember to take baskets or bowls for the collection on Sunday morning for the scholarship fund
- Keep an up-to-date list of those coming and who has paid and who has not
- Try to keep the price under $125.00 per person (with a reduced price for concessions). Alpha weekends often fill a conference center and you are therefore in a strong position to negotiate a good price.
- For those who are unable to afford the full amount, ask them to pay whatever they feel they can afford. The collection on Sunday almost always covers the amount needed
- Another possibility is to link with other churches in your area for a

joint Alpha weekend. Your Alpha Advisor might be able to help you
with organizing this
* Remember to buy a small present for the staff at the conference center
* Make a plan of where everyone is sleeping. Many centers will offer
to do this for you, but experience would suggest it is better to do it
yourself

Course Dinner – 7:00 P.M.

Dinner is an important aspect of Alpha.
People often feel more relaxed chatting over
supper. Often people have commented that
the food kept them coming back to Alpha,
so it is worth keeping the food to a good
standard!

Depending on the numbers expected,
arrange for a different group to cook supper
each week. You will know when you need a
caterer (approx 120 +). (Make sure you have
enough paper plates and cups, coffee cups,
knives, forks, tea, coffee, cookies, milk, etc.)

If you don't have a task force, the group who cooked should do the
cleaning up and clearing up. Using disposables will keep this to a
minimum.

If a group is doing the cooking, the cost can usually be kept to
approximately $3.00 per head. Put out bowls at the serving points and
reimburse whoever paid for the food. If you have a caterer, we suggest
a charge of approximately $6.00 or ask people to pay whatever they
feel they can afford. Some suggestions for Alpha meals would include
simple pasta dishes, shepherd's pie, chilli, and pizza. Make sure you
have a vegetarian alternative. Many recipes can be found in *The Alpha
Course Cookbook.*

Task force

The purpose of the Alpha task force is to provide practical services for
the Alpha course. In this way very few people from the course will

be asked to help with the more mundane tasks and will therefore not be distracted from their enjoyment of Alpha. The task force is vital to ensure that the course will run smoothly. They should be welcome to listen to the talks and should be given as much encouragement as possible. Always cherish your task force! A key appointment is the task force coordinator, who allocates the different tasks and takes pastoral care of the team.

The task force should make sure that enough Bibles and manuals are available and are ready to be handed out if necessary. Every guest should have a free manual. Place a pile of Bibles under one of the chairs in the small group. In this way, guests are not daunted by seeing Bibles on every chair (at Holy Trinity, the NIV is used). The task force should be available to help with parking cars—an important job. (Don't forget that at the beginning of the course, those helping with parking cars are the first people the guests will meet.) They also need to ensure that each group has enough chairs and that each group has a sign to identify itself. They should make sure there are spare chairs for latecomers and then at the end of the evening their job is to put away chairs. Furthermore, the task force should put out the food and set up the coffee stations. Make sure that every member of the task force has a name badge.

The task force should also run a booktable, displaying the books recommended in the *Alpha Course Manual*. Course leaders might find it helpful to become Book Agents, thereby qualifying for a discount on Alpha materials.

Alpha dinner parties

For your first Alpha course, hold a dinner party before the course starts, then hold one at the end of every course so that guests on the course can invite their friends. Appoint one person to coordinate and organize the dinner party and print some attractive invitations. These should be available from week seven for guests to give to their friends. At the same time start collecting money for the dinners. Everyone should pay for their guests as well as for themselves. Get a team together to set up the dinner and another for cleaning up at the end. These should preferably be those who are not inviting friends. Do everything possible to create a good atmosphere. Make a table plan and try to use proper plates and glasses etc. Put flowers, candles, and napkins on the table. The talk, "Is There More to Life Than This?" should come during coffee.

Questionnaires

At week nine, give each guest on the course a questionnaire (see Appendix E). This will enable you to see what God has been doing in people's lives, and will help in planning the next course. At the same time, give the group hosts a questionnaire and ask them to fill in details about every single member of their group (take the names from the address lists even if guests have not completed the course). Ask them whether their group members completed the course and, if not, do they know the reason? Ask them if their group members plan to join a home group after the course.

Keep in mind the dinner party and perhaps the guest service before the next course, ask who could give a good testimony. Ask who would be a good Alpha helper, and make sure that you remember to invite them to help on the next course.

DAYTIME COURSES
by Pippa Gumbel

Daytime Alpha is held on Wednesday mornings and was originally designed for those who were likely to find it easier to attend a course during the day rather than in the evening. There are obvious categories: people with young children, those who are self-employed or unemployed, and those who would prefer not to venture out alone at night.

The daytime Alpha course has proven as successful as the evening course as a means of evangelism. This course has seen many people come into relationship with Christ—from those very far away from Christianity, to those who want to renew their faith, or return to a faith they once knew.

Values

The daytime Alpha course promotes the same values as the evening course. The Alpha course is for anyone, regardless of life-stage or background. We try to create a friendly, relaxed atmosphere where people feel safe and valued.

Choosing the team and the helpers

We have the same priorities as an evening Alpha—choosing people who have good social skills and making people feel welcome and relaxed. We also choose people from the previous course who relate well to the guests. These people are ideal as they are only a little further along in their journey of faith and have a lot of friends outside the church. They make excellent helpers and often go on to host a group.

The numbers in the groups can be smaller than in the evening, and therefore more intimate, with two leaders and one or two helpers.

Groups

Most tend to enjoy the groups more than anything else. Some come with damaged lives from abuse of all kinds. Many need a place of peace where they can learn to accept God's forgiveness for those things they have done of which they feel ashamed, and where they can learn to trust God, and to forgive those who have hurt them.

We try to place people in a group together with others who are at the same life stage. We usually have a student group, one or two groups of guests with young children, another group of more mature guests and other groups with guests from a variety of life stages. We have a mixture of men and women on the course, although we usually have one or two groups of just women who have babies and small children. There is lots of flexibility with the group arrangements and on each course we pray that God will guide us as we place each person in a group.

Setting for daytime Alpha

Daytime Alpha works well in either a home or a church. Providing childcare is an important part of the course as we have many women who are on maternity leave, or who are full-time mothers. There needs to be sufficient room in the venue for the children to be cared for safely without disrupting the course itself.

Numbers

The course seems to work equally well whatever the numbers. We have done courses from 20 to 100 people. I have a friend who ran the course for just two friends in her home. They had a wonderful time. No course is too small.

Resources

You will need one copy of *The Alpha Course Manual* and some training manuals for the team. If you prefer to do the course by watching the DVDs then these can be purchased from alpharesources.org (in Canada davidccook.ca). Talks from the evening course can also be recommended to guests who miss a week.

Support group

It is important to be well organized and to have people from among the helpers to prepare food, serve tea and coffee, and clean up, as well as others to look after any children. We run a half hour prayer meeting before each session begins. The whole team will be committed to praying and invited to come and pray before each session. The team members with young families, who are doing school drop offs or have other commitments, are not always able to get there, but a core group pray each week. In some churches, they have an additional group who meet and pray for the course during each session.

Timing and invitations

We suggest an invitation flyer inviting people to join the daytime Alpha course, letting them know the length of the course and the schedule of the morning.

The schedule for daytime Alpha for us at Holy Trinity Brompton are:

9:45 A.M.	Breakfast
10:05 A.M.	Welcome
10:10 A.M.	Worship
10:20 A.M.	Talk
10:55 A.M.	Coffee and small groups
11:30 A.M.	Finish

Worship

Worship is introduced gradually on the course. The introductory session, "Is There More to Life Than This?", does not have any worship. This is an opportunity for people to invite friends who might be interested in coming to the course. Week one, we sign one hymn and then from week two on we sign a hymn and a contemporary song. We sing a maximum of two songs each week, except on the weekend away and the final session of the course where there might be a slightly extended time of worship.

The Alpha weekend

We invite all the guests to the Alpha weekend, which runs as part of the evening Alpha course. This is always a great success as it gives the guests an opportunity to meet new people and feel part of something bigger. However, if it is not possible to go on a weekend away, an Alpha day is a good alternative. We run an Alpha day and have also run Alpha half-days. The following programs provide examples of how to schedule an Alpha day and Alpha half-day.

Suggested Alpha day program

9:30 A.M.	Registration/coffee and muffins
10:00 A.M.	Worship
10:15 A.M.	Combined talk: "Who Is the Holy Spirit?" and "What Does the Holy Spirit Do?"
11:30 A.M.	Refreshments and small group discussions
12:30 P.M.	Talk: "How Can I Be Filled with the Holy Spirit?"
1:15 P.M.	Ministry with worship
1:45 P.M.	Lunch and group time
3:00 P.M.	Talk: "How Can I Make the Most of the Rest of My Life?"
4:30 P.M.	Finish

Suggested Alpha half-day program

9:30 A.M.	Breakfast
10:00 A.M.	Worship
10:15 A.M.	Combined talk: "Who is the Holy Spirit?" and "What Does the Holy Spirit Do?"
11:00 A.M.	Coffee break and small group discussions (1 Corinthians 12:4–11)
11:30 A.M.	Talk: "How Can I Be Filled with the Holy Spirit?"
12:10 P.M.	Ministry with worship
1:00 P.M.	Finish (optional lunch and feedback)

Daytime Alpha dinner

We join with the evening course for the Alpha celebration evening, which is an excellent setting for guests to bring their partners, friends, or family members. It gives them a wonderful opportunity to hear the gospel in a relaxed environment.

If this is not possible, a dinner in someone's home would be a good alternative.

The results of daytime Alpha

Over the years that we have been running daytime Alpha, we have seen many people coming to know Jesus and their lives being radically changed. Many are now involved in leadership at our church or in other parts of the world.

ALPHA IN THE WORKPLACE COURSES

For most of us, an average of forty hours of our time every week is spent at work. That means just over a third of our time each day is spent with our colleagues.

Have you ever found yourself wondering what your colleagues think about God? Or perhaps you are curious about their outlook on life and would love to invite them to church, yet you find it impossible to find the right opportunity to initiate or engage in a conversation in the work environment. That is why Alpha in the Workplace exists.

An Alpha in the Workplace course is designed to sandwich nicely into your normal working day. Most run in an hour either during lunch or after work when you'd normally have an end of the day meeting or share a drink with a friend or colleague. Some courses are run in your office conference room, others in a neutral venue nearby. Yet, the course retains the aspects that famously make Alpha so special: it's sociable, informative, and you'll have the opportunity to engage in discussions about the bigger questions of life with your colleagues.

Scheduling

Whatever time frame you decide on, it is important to stick to it and to finish on time. This is especially important in a workplace environment where pressure for guests to stay longer could produce tension with managers or colleagues. Whatever time frame you are working with, be encouraged! Leaders who have run Alpha in the Workplace agree that it is worth it to persist, even if you only have a short time available.

Three possible schedules

Sample program A:

Forty-five minutes

1:00 P.M.	Team arrives and sets up
1:15 P.M.	Guests arrive and start lunch
1:20 P.M.	Joke/introduction then live talk
1:40 P.M.	Small group discussion
2:00 P.M.	Finish

Sample program B:

One hour

12:50 P.M.	Team arrives and sets up
1:00 P.M.	Guests arrive and start lunch
1:05 P.M.	Joke/introduction then start *Alpha Express* DVD
1:25 P.M.	Small group discussion
2:00 P.M.	Finish

Sample program C:

One hour and fifteen minutes

12:50 P.M.	Team arrives and sets up
1:00 P.M.	Guests arrive and start lunch
1:10 P.M.	Joke/introduction then start *Alpha Express* DVD
1:30 P.M.	Finish DVD and begin small group discussion
2:15 P.M.	Finish

For further information on Alpha in the Workplace, visit alphausa.org/workplace to learn more.

* The Alpha course can be run in a variety of contexts and is suitable for any audience. Whether you're interested in hosting a moms' and tots' mid-morning course over coffee, a men's breakfast course before work, or an evening course at a local coffee shop near the office, Alpha is designed to be readily adaptable to fit your needs. We encourage you to use the example timelines we've listed for Daytime Courses (Appendix C) or Alpha in the Workplace Courses as a guide to start a course near you that will best reach people within your own community.

QUESTIONNAIRE

---

1) How did you first become aware of the Alpha course?

☐ Friend/   ☐ Banner   ☐ Cinema   ☐ Press   ☐ Other _____
    relative/   /poster   Ad/bus   /TV
    colleague   posters

2) Did you come to an Alpha dinner party before the course?

☐ Yes   ☐ No

3) Which of the following reasons best describe why you came to Alpha?
Tick all that apply:

☐ Curiosity   ☐ Spiritual search
☐ Had questions / wanted to find out more   ☐ Came with a friend
☐ Looking for meaning / purpose in life   ☐ Brought a friend / colleague /
                                              family member
                                              ☐ Other _____

4) Were you a regular churchgoer before the course?

☐ Yes   ☐ No   ☐ Occasionally

5) Are you a regular churchgoer now?

☐ Yes   ☐ No   ☐ Occasionally

6) How would you have described yourself before the course, in terms of the Christian faith?

☐ Christian   ☐ Undecided
☐ Non-Christian   ☐ Atheist
☐ Agnostic   ☐ Other _____

7) How would you describe yourself now, in terms of the Christian faith?

❐ Christian   ❐ Undecided
❐ Non-Christian   ❐ Atheist
❐ Agnostic   ❐ Other _____

8) If the answer to 6) and 7) is different, when did the change occur?

❐ Alpha Weekend / Day   ❐ Other
❐ Gradually over the course   _____

Please describe your experience:

_____

_____

_____

_____

9) In what ways, if any, did you benefit from doing the Alpha course?

Check all that apply:

❐ Discovered a relationship with God through   ❐ Made new friends
   Jesus
❐ Strengthened existing faith   ❐ Feel more love / loved
❐ Found new purpose for life   ❐ Other
                                                  _____
❐ Feel more at peace

Further comments:

_____

_____

_____

10) Which talks did you buy / download, if any?

❐ Week 1   ❐ Week 2   ❐ Week 3   ❐ Week 4   ❐ Week 5   ❐ Week 6
❐ Week 6   ❐ Week 7   ❐ Week 8   ❐ Week 9   ❐ Week 10   ❐ Alpha
                                                                           Day Talks
❐ Weekend Talks ❐ Alpha
                Day Talks

11) Which books did you buy, if any?

☐ Bible   ☐ The Screwtape Letters
☐ Searching Issues   ☐ Chasing the Dragon
☐ 30 Days   ☐ What's So Amazing about Grace?
☐ Questions of Life   ☐ The Cross and the Switchblade
☐ Mere Christianity   ☐ Other
                                            _____

12) How could the course be improved e.g., talks, small groups, weekend etc.?

_____

_____

_____

_____

_____

_____

13) Are you going to join a home group?

☐ Yes   ☐ No   ☐ Maybe

If Yes, which one? _____

14) Will you be attending church?

☐ Yes   ☐ No   ☐ Maybe

If Yes, which one? _____

_____

15) Would you like to find out more about the work of Alpha?

☐ Yes   ☐ No

16) Any other comments:

_____

_____

_____

_____

_____

HOW TO AVOID THE SEVEN COMMON MISTAKES

Research has revealed seven common mistakes that people make when running an Alpha course, which can prevent it from being a truly effective form of evangelism. The way to avoid these mistakes is to follow the seven key steps outlined below.

1. Aim to attend an Alpha conference

Running Alpha without attending a conference is like driving a car without taking any lessons. We have found that those churches whose course leaders attend a conference experience a far higher degree of success with their Alpha course.

It may be that the Alpha course leaders who first made the decision to run Alpha in your church have now handed the responsibility to others. In this case, the new team will benefit from attending an Alpha conference. The aims of the Alpha conference are as follows:

• To explain the theological and practical reasons for running Alpha
• To share with others what we have learned over the last twenty years from our own mistakes
• To provide all the practical training needed to run an effective Alpha course
• To consider the importance of:
  worship
  services
  talks (including a model Alpha evening)
  prayer ministry
  small group training
• To provide opportunities for prayer ministry

If you have never been to a conference, we would be delighted if you would consider attending the next Alpha conference in your area or one of the two conferences held at Holy Trinity Brompton each year. Most course leaders have found it valuable to bring their leadership team with them to establish a sense of unity in purpose and vision. Details of Alpha conferences can be found in *Alpha News* or on the Alpha website: alpha.org (If for some reason you are unable to attend a conference, the *Principles and Practicalities of Alpha* video content is available at alpha.org)

2. Think about your team carefully

It is vital to get the right people hosting and helping on your Alpha course. The right team transforms a course and directly affects the number of guests attending Alpha.

What makes the right team?
Hosts and helpers on Alpha should be positive, outgoing people who relate well to those outside the church. There is a simple test for good hosts and helpers. Ask yourself: "Would I happily put my closest friend who is not a Christian in that person's group?"

How to avoid burnout
Keep renewing your Alpha team. It is important to keep an eye out for new people you can invite to join your team. Guests from your last course often make very good helpers and their faith is likely to grow as they help in a group. Those most reluctant to be helpers can be the best ones, as they identify well with new guests. Even those relatively new to the faith can make excellent group hosts. Always be looking for potential hosts in your congregation.

Remember to delegate to your team
Look out for other people's gifts and don't be afraid to use them. This will prevent you from becoming exhausted and will enable them to develop their talents. Some people are natural group hosts. Others love to serve by cooking, setting up, welcoming, and so on. These are the people best suited to join the taskforce for your course. In larger courses the taskforce might even form their own small group.

3. Stay in training

Alpha team training

Hosting an Alpha group is very different from leading any other type of church small group. On Alpha the emphasis is on group discussions and participation rather than playing the role of "teacher." The host acts more as a "facilitator."

The Alpha Team Training consists of three talks: "Hosting Small Groups," "Pastoral Care," and "Ministry." The first two training sessions should be held on the two weeks prior to the start of the course. We meet at 7:00 P.M. for dinner so that the team can get to know each other before the course begins. We move on to worship and prayer at 7:30 P.M. All the way through we stress the importance of praying for the course. We then have a talk and an opportunity to ask questions relating to the talk or any other aspect of the course. We then cover administrative details and recommended reading before the start of the course (*Questions of Life*) and try to finish by 9:30 P.M. The ministry training session takes place during the week before the weekend away and follows the same format. These three talks are available on DVD, and a manual is also available. We also recommend that the team reads *Searching Issues* and *Telling Others: How to Run the Alpha Course*.

It is essential that you train each member of your Alpha team every time you run the course. Even those who have led on Alpha before will find it valuable, both to refresh their memory and to meet others who are helping on that course. The sessions also provide an opportunity to pray for the course.

The principles of Alpha

Experience shows that it is vital for teams to understand not just the "whats" and "hows," but also the "whys" of Alpha—the principles of the course. The ideal way to achieve this is to take the core members of your team to an Alpha conference, which covers both the principles and the practicalities of the Alpha course. However, if this is not possible, consider showing *How to Run the Alpha Course* (which covers the talks on principles and practicalities) to your team once a year. This content is available free online at alpha.org.

4. Follow the recipe

Alpha is tried and tested and it has been running in a wide range of settings for more than twenty years. Every ingredient has been included for a very important reason. Those courses that leave out one ingredient, such as the meal, diminish the impact of Alpha.

For example:

- The meal is an essential element, enabling guests to relax, friendships to form, and groups to gel.
- The weekend or day away allows guests to look at the person and work of the Holy Spirit in a relaxed setting, giving them time to think through what they have heard or experienced.
- It is vital to give the guests the opportunity to respond and to be ministered to during the weekend.
- The healing night is a time when amazing things often happen. We have found that people are often more open to the Holy Spirit at this point than they are at the weekend.
- Including worship week by week helps to prepare the guests for the weekend. Some churches have found it helpful to use CDs because they do not have musicians.

5. Don't forget the weekend away

We highly recommend a weekend away. However, if only a day away is possible, that too will be effective. It is important to have one or the other and not to miss out the talks on the person and work of the Holy Spirit.

A survey carried out by the Methodist Church found a direct correlation between churches that left out the talks on the Holy Spirit and those that were disappointed with their Alpha course. The work of the Holy Spirit is crucial to Alpha and giving the guests an opportunity to be prayed for is a vital part of the course. Time and again God has honored simple requests for Him to send His Spirit among us—with profound changes often occurring in people's lives as a result. It is only through the work of the Spirit that we are able to see people give their lives to Christ, be filled with the Spirit, get excited about Jesus, and bring their friends to the next course.

If you need any help with your weekend or day away, contact your Alpha Advisor, who can give advice or even arrange for a team to come and help you. (There is a list of Alpha Advisors in *Alpha News* or online at alphafriends.org/advisers) You might also consider running an Alpha weekend or day away with other churches in your area.

6. Invite people from outside the church

Experience has shown that most of the guests on the first Alpha course run by a church are from the congregation. The second course may well be smaller, and again the majority of guests may be congregation members. By the third course there will be far fewer congregation members (as most of those interested will have come on the first or second course), and there will probably be one or two guests from outside the church. That's fantastic because Alpha is primarily designed for nonchurchgoers. The more nonChristians you have on your course, the more comfortable your guests will feel about exploring the Christian faith. The important thing is for the congregation to keep inviting their friends to Alpha. This keeps the balance tipped towards those outside the church with guests often inviting their friends, family, and colleagues to the next course, thus further widening the pool of guests.

7. Keep Alpha rolling

Alpha is a long-term strategy which, when run well over an extended period, leads to a constant stream of new people. Experience has shown that churches who persevere with running Alpha three times a year in this way, even when their numbers on the course are reducing, find that they experience growth in the long run.

PRAYER AND ALPHA

Pastor Dutch Sheets wrote: "Evangelism without prayer is like a grenade without a detonator. Prayer without evangelism is like a detonator without a grenade." Prayer lies at the heart of the success of any Alpha course and many churches have testified to the dramatic improvement in the success of their course when they have started to pray for it. There are five situations where praying for Alpha is particularly appropriate.

1. Hosts and helpers pray for the individuals in their small group

As well as committing to the ten weeks of the Alpha course and the weekend away, the Alpha hosts and helpers are responsible for praying regularly for the guests in their group, ideally daily during personal prayer time. We recommend that two hosts and two helpers are recruited to look after eight guests, so each host and helper may like to take responsibility for praying for two guests. The hosts and helpers are in the best position to pray as they are aware of the needs of each individual as the Alpha course progresses.

2. Hosts and helpers pray together for their small group

In addition, the hosts and helpers of each small group can meet together, maybe before church on Sunday or some other suitable time, to pray for the course. This will help to unite the leadership team of the small group and to reinforce the individual prayer referred to above.

3. Hosts and helpers pray together immediately prior to the course

It is helpful for the whole Alpha team to meet each week before the guests arrive for a team briefing and prayer meeting. The items for prayer are largely self-defining, e.g., the weekend away, the Alpha celebration dinners, etc. This is particularly important for the session "Does God Heal Today?", as the team can wait on the Lord for words of knowledge, pictures, and so on. These can then be read out after the talk and people who respond to them can be offered prayer.

4. Prayer in Week 5 "Why and How Do I Pray?"

During the session "Why and How Do I Pray?" guests are given a theology, model, and practice for prayer. This relates primarily to personal prayer, which is a good starting point as people come into relationship with God. As prayer establishes itself in people's lives it should be possible to start praying together in the small group. Do not try to introduce prayer to the small group until the end of this session at the earliest. You may find that your group is not ready to pray together until after the sessions on the Holy Spirit. If possible try to pray together at least once prior to the talk "Does God Heal Today?"

Tips for praying together in the small groups

Don't rush this! Be sensitive to where people are spiritually. If you are going to open the session in prayer then we suggest saying something like, "I have asked John to open in prayer" so that the other guests will not be afraid that the host might ask them to pray without giving notice at some time in the future. Remember that praying out loud for the first time can be quite an intimidating experience.

When you feel that the group is ready to pray, suggest that the group splits into triplets of all men or all women to pray. This makes it easier for people. The faith of the small group can be built up by feeding back answers to prayer.

When you start to pray in the small group, don't pray your longest and most eloquent prayer. The guests will feel that they could never do that—and then they won't! Pray a short, simple prayer and the guests will be encouraged to think, "Well, I could do better than that"—and then they will!

One of the hosts or helpers should refrain from praying, showing the group that it is all right not to pray aloud.

5. Praying for Alpha as a church

While it is important that those who are hosting and helping on Alpha are praying for the course, we also try to encourage the whole church to pray for the Alpha course. We have found that an open corporate prayer meeting held weekly on a different day to the Alpha course works well. The agenda covers all areas of the life of the church, but one of the regular items is prayer for evangelism and Alpha. This weekly prayer meeting is an integral part of church life and incorporates times of worship.

Anna Davies has run a number of Alpha courses in Weston-super-Mare. She writes:

> We had put a lot of effort into trying to run the past few Alpha courses really well but had seen very little come of it by way of new Christians being born. However, the prayer meetings, which began nine months ago, have provided an opportunity for more united, consistent prayer for Alpha, and we are now seeing on this present Alpha course a significant change. Nearly every one of the twenty-four people on the course is not a Christian and there is an atmosphere of genuine openness to the gospel. We are aware of God being more present in a way that He has not been before and, very importantly, He seems to be peeling off some of the things in our own lives that hinder us from being effective communicators of the gospel.

WORSHIP ON ALPHA

"Speak to one another with psalms, hymns and spiritual songs. Sing and make music in your heart to the Lord, always giving thanks to God the Father for everything, in the name of our Lord Jesus Christ" (Ephesians 5:19–20).

The practicalities of introducing worship on the Alpha course

1. Why is worship an integral part of the Alpha course?

Worship is at the heart of a relationship with God. Men and women have been created by Him to worship, whether they choose to do so or not. We are encouraged to worship God with the whole of our lives (Romans 12:1). Any practical introduction to the Christian faith must include teaching about worshiping God. The Alpha course does this by helping the guests to experience it first-hand.

Music plays a significant part in worship. Throughout the Bible, we are encouraged to express our worship, especially corporately, by using our voices and by playing instruments. When we worship we experience God's presence (Psalm 145:18; 2 Chronicles 5:13–14) and people may be converted
(cf. Acts 16:25–30; Psalm 40:3).

Throughout Alpha, guests are invited to participate in worship by singing with a worship leader and, ultimately, by putting their trust in Jesus Christ. The last talk on the weekend away stresses the need to give the whole of our lives to God. Corporately, this giving of ourselves may be expressed through the times of worship on each evening of the course.

2. The experience of worship on Alpha

Although at the beginning many find the worship the most difficult part of Alpha, by the end it is generally the most appreciated time.

One guest who wasn't a Christian at the beginning of the course said, "The singing on the first night was terrifying." Yet by the end of the course, when asked what was most enjoyed, he said, "The singing—I feel like my voice has a purpose! I hardly ever got the chance to sing before. It's great to sing and really mean the words."

Why is it so difficult? Most people in today's culture do not sing very often, apart from perhaps in the shower or at a soccer match. It is therefore a little optimistic to expect uninhibited praise on the first night. It is important not to compound the situation further by singing personal statements of faith (i.e., songs that express personal experience such as "I Love You Lord") too early in the course. For those who are wary of singing in public, it is even more difficult to sing something they do not believe.

In today's culture, there is unfortunately a perceived stigma attached to some church music. It is seen as out of date, boring, or embarrassing. Many come to church for the first time with this perception in the back of their mind. If we are going to use worship on Alpha, it is important to challenge this perception and prove it wrong. As with everything else on the course we have tried to follow the maxim: "Strive for excellence or don't do it at all."

Why is it so appreciated? As guests find faith, worshiping God becomes a natural desire. Music is a wonderful expression of this desire.

Part of the vision for Alpha is to demonstrate what church is like. Worship music is an aspect of typical church life. Learning how to worship God and being familiar with the hymns and songs that we usually sing helps guests to integrate into our church at the end of the course. Worship becomes for many a first experience of communicating with God. It helps to develop an understanding of what God is like: real, awesome, loving, and approachable.

3. How to do it

Although worship should always be Christ-centered, we try to bear in mind that the Alpha course as a whole is a ministry to the guest. Therefore we aim to introduce worship both gradually and sensitively. Here are a few pointers that might help.

Time. On the first night, we sing two songs, which lasts about five minutes in total. For the first few weeks the time of worship is kept short to enable guests to get used to singing. An extra song may be added as appropriate. At the weekend, guests are encouraged to worship for longer, with up to five or six songs at each session. As guests find faith, their enthusiasm for worship seems to increase, and times of worship lasting twenty minutes become the norm for the rest of the course.

Song choice. There is a suggested song list at the end of this Appendix. In addition, you may like to use other hymns and songs that you already use in your church.

Song choice should initially favor objective truth: songs of universal fact about the unchanging all-powerful nature of God. Be sensitive to unbelieving guests early on the course, avoiding songs such as "I Believe in Jesus" or "I Love You Lord." These songs presume faith and must be owned before they can be sung with integrity. As guests begin to allow God to integrate objective truth and personal experience, so worship times will begin to reflect their deepening faith and intimacy with God.

Be sure to have the correct copyright licenses for using songs on sheets or projecting the words on a screen. Details are given at the end of this Appendix.

What to expect on the night. Initially, many in the group will not sing, and those who do will probably not sing very loudly. It can therefore feel uncomfortable for those leading. Try to keep these things in mind:

* Don't worry if it feels like a performance. Truth is being sung whether the congregation joins in or not (see Isaiah 55:10–11).
* Be patient. Consider what it must be like for the newcomer. There is

plenty of time for what you may consider true worship to develop.
- A key governing principle of the Alpha course as a whole is the
  respect for the individual (see 1 Peter 3:15). Don't force guests to do
  anything that they feel uncomfortable with. Rather say, "Please just
  be yourself, stand or sit, sing or don't sing; do whatever you feel
  like." Emphasize the scriptural encouragement to "make music in
  your heart" (Ephesians 5:19), which is where true worship lies.
- Encourage every team member and host to be sensitive and to
  moderate their worshiping fervor! The whole Alpha evening, and
  therefore the time of worship, is primarily a ministry to the guest,
  not the host or helper. It is vital that the guests feel as comfortable as
  possible and are not distracted by what they might consider unusual
  actions on the part of the hosts and helpers.
- Clapping, raising hands, using percussion, and other such activities
  are difficult for many at first because they appear to be odd behavior.
  If and when these elements are introduced, explain why they're
  done—they're not part of some bizarre ritual, but rooted in Scripture
    – Clapping and shouting—Psalm 47:1
    – Dancing, tambourine, and instruments—Psalm 150
    – Lifting hands—1 Timothy 2:8; Psalm 63:4; Lamentations
      3:41

Having said all of this, the authentic worship of the team is vital
and often touches the guests as they witness a genuine enjoyment of
worshiping God.

4. Alpha worship leaders: characteristics and skills

We have always appointed a worship leader to take responsibility
for the music on the course. We have found it helpful to pray for the
right person to lead, taking into account, where possible, the following
characteristics:

A desire to worship God. The ruling passion in any worship leader's
heart should be to enjoy worshiping God, both individually and in the
church context. This desire then overflows into the leadership of others
so that they too may enjoy God in this way.

A lifestyle of worship. 'The Lord does not look at the things people look at. Human beings look at the outward appearance, "but the Lord looks at the heart" (1 Samuel 16:7). Worship is about the whole of our lives being orientated towards God. Our motives and actions must match the sentiments expressed in the songs.

A servant heart. Any ministry is one of service—serving God, the body of Christ and those in authority. It is vital that the worship leader is open to ideas, suggestions and, if necessary, correction. Humility is the key to successful leadership (see Mark 10:43–45).

Musical ability. The following points are things to aim for if you are selecting a worship leader:

- He or she should ideally be able to play a "lead" instrument, e.g. guitar or piano, to a reasonable standard. If they do not, they should have a close rapport with a guitarist or pianist so that the music gives a clear lead to the guests.
- It is helpful for the leader to have a strong singing voice with good intonation.
- Even and consistent rhythmic ability is essential.
- They should aim to have a thorough knowledge of the songs and their various styles.
- A professional background in music can sometimes be a hindrance rather than a help as a worship leader is not a performer. In fact, he or she needs to be full of humility, willing to decrease and let Jesus increase (John 3:30).
- If there are a number of musicians, time should be taken to arrange songs in rehearsals ahead of time.
- An eye for detail is useful, e.g. ensuring that songbooks and chord sheets are available; that all the instruments are in tune; that the musicians' area is tidy. This inspires confidence in the musicians and the guests.
- Full preparation, practice, and prayer will free the leader and the guests to be relaxed.

Musical attitude.
- The worship leader should keep his or her eyes open during the

songs. Eye contact encourages the guests and enables the leader to see the extent to which they are involved in worshiping.
- Smile. It is a wonderful privilege and joy to worship God.
- Only the worship leader leads the worship. Prayerfully work out the song list beforehand, stick to it and don't be subject to having to sing the favorite songs of individuals. It's a good thing, and far from unholy or "Spirit-quenching," to plan ahead.
- The worship leader only leads the worship! Just play and sing the songs. Do not stop between songs to give mini sermons. Let it flow.

Alpha suggested song list

It must be stressed that the songs listed below are only ideas. Feel free to experiment and find what works best for you.

Week 1	O Lord My God
	How Great is Our God
Week 2	Amazing Grace
	How Great is Our God
Week 3	O Lord My God
	Everlasting God
Week 4	Everlasting God
	I Stand Amazed
Week 5	How Great is Our God
	I Stand Amazed
Week 6	Mighty to Save
	When I Survey
Week 7	O Lord My God
	Mighty to Save
Weekend away	
	O Lord My God
	Happy Day
	Blessed be Your Name
	Love Came Down
	Mighty to Save
	How Great is Our God
	The Stand
	This is Our God

	This is My Desire
	I Stand Amazed
	Remain
	When I Survey
	All Glory
	Glory in the Highest
	Faithful One
Week 8	Blessed be Your Name
	How Great is Our God
	Here I Am to Worship
Week 9	O Lord My God
	Mighty to Save
	When I Survey
Week 10	Everlasting God
	This is Our God
	I Stand Amazed
Week 11	Blessed be Your Name
	Everlasting God
	Amazing Grace

Copyright license details

If you wish to reproduce song words or copy/print songsheets, you must have a CCL license. This may be obtained from:

Christian Copyright Licensing Ltd
Chantry House
22 Upperton Road
Eastbourne
East Sussex
BN21 1BF
Tel: 01323 417711
Email: info@ccli.co.uk

U.S.A.
CCLI
17201 NE Sacramento Street
Portland
Oregon 97230
Tel: +503 257 2230
Fax: +503 257 2244

South Africa
CCLI (Pty) Ltd.
PO Box 2347
Durbanville 7551
South Africa
Tel: +27 21 914 8908

Scandinavia
CCLI
Bärnstensvägen 37
907 41 UMEÅ
Sweden
Tel: +46 90 190 110

Australia
CCLI
PO Box 6644
Baulkham Hills BC, NSW 2153
Australia
Tel: +61 2 9894 5386

New Zealand
CCLI
PO Box 210012
Laurence Stevens Drive
Manukau 2154, Auckland
New Zealand
Tel: Auckland: +9 887 0390
    Christchurch: +3 667 0258
    Wellington: +4 887 0252

For more information, visit ccli.com/Global.aspx

ALPHA WEEKEND ENTERTAINMENT

Organizer's instructions

The entertainment is a crucial part of the Alpha weekend and is a great way of breaking down barriers and unifying the group. However, it is also a potential disaster area if it goes on too long or if some of the material is inappropriate.

The role of the organizer of the entertainment is to raise everyone's enthusiasm for the entertainment, encouraging people/groups to contribute acts and to collect the acts, ensuring that each act is in line with the pointers below. It sometimes takes a lot of tact to deal with difficult people who want to do an act that may be unsuitable. It is important to be kind but firm. The last part of the job is to emcee the evening—linking up all the acts and rallying the audience.

Here are some pointers to help the evening go smoothly:

- There should be nothing with a religious focus or subject matter
- There should be nothing with unhelpful innuendo
- There should be no in-jokes
- We suggest about ten acts/skits/musical pieces in total
- The entertainment should last approximately one hour in total
- Keep a record of any acts that you thought worked particularly well, for possible future use
- If you have any problems or doubts always ask the director or the leader of the weekend.

ENDNOTES

Chapter 1

1. *Daily Mail*, January 13, 2004.
2. From the Church of England website, January 13, 2004: www.ceo.anglican.org/cgi-bin/news.
3. Statistics from *1992 Social Trends* from the Central Statistical Office, and also http://www.statistics.gov. uk/cci/nscl.asp?id=7476 and http://www.dh.gov.uk/en/ Publicationsandstatistics/Publications/ PublicationsStatistics/ DH_116039.
4. Leading missiologist David Bosch defines evangelism as the proclamation of salvation in Christ to those who do not believe in Him, calling them to repentance and conversion, announcing forgiveness of sin, inviting them to become living members of Christ's earthly community, and to begin a life of service to others in the power of the Holy Spirit.
5. John Stott, *The Contemporary Christian* (IVP, 1992), p. 241.
6. Benedict XVI, Homily, August 21, 2005.
7. Michael Green, *Evangelism Through the Local Church* (Hodder & Stoughton, 1990), p. ix.
8. John Stott, *The Contemporary Christian* (IVP, 1992), pp.121, 127.
9. Graham Tomlin, in R. T. France and A. E. McGrath (eds), *Evangelical Anglicans* (SPCK, 1993), pp. 82–95.
10. Pope John Paul II. Commissioning Families, Neo-Catechumenal way. January 3, 1991.
11. Pope Paul VI in Evangelii Nuntianti Apostolic Exaltation on Evangelisation in the Modern World, December 8, 1975.
12. John Stott, *Issues Facing Christians Today* (Marshalls, 1984), p. xi.
13. Lesslie Newbigin, *The Open Secret* (SPCK, 1995), p. 11.
14. Wayne Grudem, *Systematic Theology* (IVP, 1994), pp. 763–787.
15. W. Reginald Ward and Richard P. Heitzenrater (eds). The Works of John Wesley. Vol.19, Journals and Diaries (1738–43) (Abingdon press. 1990).

16. David Pawson, *Fourth Wave* (Hodder & Stoughton, 1993), pp. 36–37.
17. John Pollock, *John Wesley* (Hodder & Stoughton, 1989), p. 118.
18. George Whitefield's *Journal* (Banner of Truth, 1992).
19. Charles Finney, *Memoirs of Rev. Charles G. Finney* (Fleming H. Revell, 1876), p. 19.
20. John Pollock, *Moody without Sankey* (Hodder & Stoughton, 1963), pp. 83, 87.
21. R. A. Torrey, *The Baptism with the Holy Spirit* (Dimension Books, 1972), pp. 11, 54.
22. R. A. Torrey. *Why God Used D. L. Moody* (Kessinger Publishing LLC, 2006)
23. John Pollock, *Billy Graham* (Hodder & Stoughton, 1966), pp. 62–63.
24. *The Word Among Us*, daily meditations for May 1996, "A Pentecost Retreat with Fr. Raniero Cantalamessa, Preacher to the Papal Household".

Chapter 3

1. G. K. Chesterton, *Orthodoxy* (Serenity Publishers, 2009).
2. Robert W. Jenson, *Systematic Theology*, vol. 2, *The Works of God* (Oxford University Press, 1999) p. 185, cited by Colin Gunton, *The Christian Faith* (Blackwell Publishers, 2002), p. 9.
3. Nicky Gumbel, *Questions of Life* (Kingsway, 1993).

Chapter 5

1. Nicky Gumbel, *Why Jesus?* (Kingsway, 1991).

Chapter 7

1. Nicky Gumbel, *Searching Issues* (Kingsway, 1994).

Chapter 9

1. Juan Carlos Ortiz, quoted in *Alpha* Magazine, January 1993.
2. R. A. Torrey, *Personal Work* (Pickering & Inglis, 1974), pp. 9–10.

Chapter 11
1. *Church Times*, September 7, 1989.
2. C. H. Spurgeon, *Lectures to My Students* (Marshall Pickering, 1954), p. 77.
3. Phillips Brooks, *Lectures on Preaching: The Yale Lectures* (Dutton, 1877; Allenson, 1895; Baker, 1969), p. 28.

Chapter 13
1. *The New Bible Dictionary* (IVP, 1962), p. 827.

Alpha USA
1635 Emerson Lane
Naperville, IL 60540

800.362.5742
+ 212.406.5269

info@alphausa.org
alphausa.org
alpharesources.org

@alphausa

Alpha in the Caribbean
Holy Trinity Brompton
Brompton Road
London SW7 1JA UK

+44 (0) 845.644.7544

americas@alpha.org
caribbean.Alpha.org

@AlphaCaribbean

Alpha Canada
Suite #230
11331 Coppersmith Way
Richmond, BC V7A 5J9

800.743.0899

office@alphacanada.org
alphacanada.org

Purchase resources in Canada:

David C. Cook Distribution
Canada
P.O. Box 98, 55 Woodslee Avenue
Paris, ON N3L 3E5

800.263.2664

custserve@davidccook.ca
davidccook.ca

Available wherever Christian books are sold.

What is Alpha?

Alpha is a series of sessions exploring the Christian faith, typically run over eleven weeks. Each talk looks at a different question around faith and is designed to create conversation. Alpha is run all around the world, and everyone is welcome.

Find out more
alphausa.org | alphacanada.org | caribbean.alpha.org

"Alpha was the best thing I ever did. It helped answer some huge questions and find a simple, empowering faith in my life."
Bear Grylls, Adventurer

Global Alpha Stats
169 countries | 29 million guests | 81 languages

What to expect

A typical Alpha

Alpha runs in cafés, churches, universities, homes, bars—you name it. No two Alphas look the same, but they generally have three key things in common: food, a talk and good conversation.

Alpha Topics

Alpha explores the following topics over 11 weeks, including a weekend or day away. We recommend beginning and ending each Alpha with a party where guests can invite their friends who might be interested in attending the next Alpha. Alpha is free of charge to guests.

Session 1:   Is There More to Life Than This?
Session 2:   Who is Jesus?
Session 3:   Why Did Jesus Die?
Session 4:   How Can We Have Faith?
Session 5:   Why and How Do I Pray?
Session 6:   Why and How Should I Read the Bible?
Session 7:   How Does God Guide Us?

Alpha Weekend or Day Away

Session 8:   Who is the Holy Spirit?
Session 9:   What Does the Holy Spirit Do?
Session 10:   How Can I Be Filled with the Holy Spirit?
Session 11:   How Can I Make the Most of the Rest of My Life?

Session 12:   How Can I Resist Evil?
Session 13:   Why and How Should I Tell Others?
Session 14:   Does God Heal Today?
Session 15:   What About the Church?

Connect with Alpha

Let's connect
We welcome any opportunity to speak with you. Whether it's hearing your vision, or simply assisting you with a question, our team is waiting to talk with you.

alphausa.org/contact
800.362.5742

alphacanada.org/connect
800.743.0899

carribean.alpha.org/contact
868.671.0133

Tell us your story
Has your life been changed on Alpha? We would love to hear how God worked in your life. It might be just what someone considering attending Alpha needs to hear to take that next step.

Share your story:
USA: #MyAlphaStory
Canada: stories@alphacanada.org

Go deeper in the Word
Start your day with the Bible in One Year, a free Bible reading app with commentary by Nicky and Pippa Gumbel. Receive a daily email or audio commentary coordinated with the Bible in One Year reading plan.

alpha.org/bioy

Join our online communities
Looking for like-minded people who are talking about their recent experience on Alpha? Join the conversation on social media.

Find us on Facebook.
Twitter - @alphausa; @alphacanada; @alphalatam
Instagram - @alphausa | #RunAlpha

Getting started with Alpha

PREPARE: We're here to help you
We are eager to help you get your Alpha started. Contact us to connect with a network of experienced Alpha coaches and leaders in your local region.

PLAN: Go online to build your Alpha
Within Alpha Builder you will find team training videos and resources both for you and for your Alpha team. Oh, did we mention they are all free?

It's crucial that you make sure that all of your hosts, helpers and other team members are trained. Alpha small groups are different from other small groups that they may have participated in before, so they need to know how to run their group well.

PROMOTE: Easily promote your Alpha with our tools
Easily promote your Alpha by customizing our tools within Alpha Builder. You can post your Alpha on our website so guests can find you online. You can also download free resources to invite guests to your next Alpha. In the USA you can also find many promotional tools in our print shop at alpharesources.org

PRAY: Lay the right foundation
Prayer is the foundation of Alpha. Gather a team to pray and go for it. You are part of a global story and we cannot wait to hear how it goes.

"What if I told you that Alpha is the most predictably redemptive tool I've ever seen in 40 years of ministry? Would you pilot one Alpha group in your church?"

Bill Hybels, Senior Pastor of Willow Creek Community Church

One Alpha, three ways to run

The Alpha Film Series
Begin the greatest adventure with us. The Alpha Film Series is an updated, relevant and engaging way to experience the Alpha talks. They are designed to take the audience on an epic journey exploring the basics of the Christian faith.

Alpha with Nicky Gumbel
Alpha pioneer Nicky Gumbel delivers a complete set of 29-minute Alpha talks for a new generation. Filmed live at HTB, London, this DVD provides the timeless version of Alpha talks for tens of thousands of churches of all denominations around the world (contains subtitles).

The Alpha Youth Film Series
Twelve video sessions filmed all around the globe, designed to engage students and young people in conversations about faith, life and Jesus. Available online for free or for purchase as a DVD or flashdrive.

Related Alpha resources

Introduction to Alpha Sampler
This kit will provide you with five important resources to review and expand your understanding of how to run Alpha.

Alpha Toolkit
The Alpha Toolkit will help you to plan and run your Alpha. With enough materials for 10 guests, it also provides training materials, the main talk video, team and guest resources, and more.

Searching Issues
Nicky Gumbel tackles the seven most common objections to the Christian faith, including suffering,other religions. Recommended reading for all small group hosts and helpers.

Alpha Guide
Essential for every Alpha guest, the guide serves as a companion to the talks. The guide is an invaluable resource to guests during Alpha and as a reference for individual reflection long after Alpha is over.